Coresponsibility in the Church

Coresponsibility in the Church

Léon-Joseph Cardinal Suenens

Translated by Francis Martin

Herder and Herder

1968
HERDER AND HERDER NEW YORK
232 Madison Avenue, New York 10016

Original edition: *Co-responsabilité dans l'église d'aujourd'hui,*
Bruges, Desclée De Brouwer, 1968.

Nihil obstat: Thomas J. Beary, Censor Librorum
Imprimatur: ✠Robert F. Joyce, Bishop of Burlington
May 2, 1968

Library of Congress Catalog Card Number: 68–29409
© 1968 by Léon-Joseph Cardinal Suenens
Manufactured in the United States

CONTENTS

Coresponsibility in the Church

Preface

In the wake of Vatican II, the church is questioning itself about its own nature, and about its mission within a world in the process of being born. Many questions arise exercising a mutual influence upon one another. Within this vast complex of problems, some priorities can be discerned, and in these pages I have tried to draw out that which on the level of pastoral activity seems to be the dominating theme of the council: the coresponsibility of all Christians within the people of God. Coresponsibility is embodied at all times in ecclesiastical institutions, but, institutionalized or not, it is always underlying the very life of the church. This synthetic aspect of collegial notion will occupy most of our attention.

In the first part, after having located the church in its historical context on the morrow of Vatican II, we will attempt to point out what seem to be the great demands of the moment: the ecumenical urgency, the mission urgency, and the urgency for the church to be present to the world. We are all summoned to this threefold task, each one according to his proper function and charism, but all in close solidarity.

In the second part, we will consider coresponsibility actualized in regard to the papacy, bishops, priests, theologians, deacons, the religious and the laity. However, a listing such as this implies no value judgment. We are well aware that in the people of God, functions, offices, ministries, states of life and charisms are organically bound together in a complex network of structural lines and living relationships (*Dogmatic Constitution on the Church,* art. 13). But in order that our suggestions be specific and the text more readable, some kind of divisions have to be made in the subject matter: there seems to be no way of avoiding this. The greater part of our attention will be concentrated upon those things which will help us translate the texts of Vatican II into practical realization within the daily life of the church.

This English translation, whose text I have seen in manuscript, includes some additions made during the process of preparing the book for publication.

The only goal of these pages is to aid in a growing awareness of the fact that the church is a mystery of communion, and that the pastoral effort of tomorrow will spring forth from the very heart of our faith as lived out within this profound reality of the church.

PART ONE

The Church Today

I.

The Church in the Period Following Vatican II

Vatican II in Relation to the Past

The Second Vatican Council marked the end of an epoch. Or if one wishes to look back even further, it marked the end of a series of epochs. It signified the end of an era.

We could say that in a certain way, it closed the age of Constantine, the age of medieval Christianity, the era of Counter-reformation, the period of Vatican I. In the context of its ancient past, it marks a turning point in the history of the Church.

On the other hand, in the context of its more immediate past, that is, the first half of our century, it appears not so much as a terminal point as a synthesis. Vatican II was the heir and beneficiary of those great movements of renewal which were and are stirring in the heart of the modern church; we mean the biblical, liturgical, patristic, theological and pastoral renewals.

13

The council caught and channeled these currents, and, under the influence of the Spirit, made of them mighty rivers whose strong flow caused the waters to penetrate deeply into the heart of the sea. When he opened the council, John XXIII desired that it be a springtime for the Church; his wish and his hope were amply fulfilled. But as with every springtime, the renewal of the Church experiences some unseasonable weather.

There is no denying it: because they did not notice the slow theological maturing of the last thirty years, and were not aware of the rising sap which the council perceived and diffused in many directions, many of the faithful were confused by certain breaks with the past. They were surprised by the debates at the council which questioned certitudes and practices once considered classic, and which, all at once, presented a welter of problems under a light that seemed to distort them.

It is difficult for such people to distinguish the unchangeable religious Tradition of the Church from human or sociological traditions which, though they may be ancient, have but a peripheral or accidental relation to the faith.

In growing things, the full potential of springtime is never reached except at the price of a certain pruning; but the pruning shears and saw must be handled wisely. It is difficult to look at a tree, newly cut and shorn of its branches, and believe that this bare thing will give birth to a renewal of life; that from this winter, spring will come.

As the years go on, we will see ever more clearly that Vatican II was a council of the greatest importance. We will understand that it pruned away some foliage only to allow the tree to blossom.

14

Vatican II in Relation to the Future

However, to grasp the full meaning of the council, it is not enough to view it only in relation to a past which it concludes. We must also consider it in the light of those forces of the future which it contains. It is, in its own turn, a point of departure, as Pope Paul VI forcefully reminds us.

The conciliar decrees are not so much a destination as a point of departure toward new goals. The renewing power and spirit of the council must continue to penetrate to the very depths of the church's life. The seeds of life planted by the council in the soil of the church must grow and achieve full maturity.[1]

These words invite us, in our present moment, to see Vatican II in its relation to the future. The church is a church on the way, a pilgrim church. It never has the right to stop; it pauses only to prepare itself for new steps on its journey. Under certain aspects the church is always "passing." John XXIII used to love to say, "They speak of me as a transition pope," and then he would add, "That is true, but the continuity of the Church is made from transition to transition."

Henri Bergson once wrote, "What has struck me about Jesus is precisely this mandate to go on always toward the future. So much so that it could be said that the stable element of Christianity is the order never to stop."

Whether we wish it or not, we are at the moment en route towards some Vatican III, whose character must remain vague and which will take place in a tomorrow as yet

1. Letter of Paul VI to International Theological Congress of Rome, September 21, 1966.

undefinable. This Vatican III will have to discern and strengthen that which Vatican II possesses only as seed, as potential, as riches for the future.

Commenting on our Lord's phrase, "I will build my church," Pope Paul VI developed the image of a church still being constructed.

We want to invite you to do a little thinking about the force of the expression used by Christ: "I will build." This expression shows the Lord's permanent action regarding his church. It shows the dynamic character which the life of the church, as represented in a building under construction, assumes. It indicates the continuous development laid down for the church by virtue of the notion of a labor which must be carried on according to a positive, visible plan drawn up by Christ himself, and not left to the whim and imagination of the workers. The church must be built. It is always an incomplete building which continues its fixed plan of execution throughout time.

If we keep in mind that Christ's activity, since his ascension, is carried out in accordance with his divine command by the church itself, by those in the church who have the function of promoting and continuing the work of Jesus, then this concept of the church being perfected becomes very enlightening for us. It becomes a program if we reflect that we are all called to participate in this positive, mystical work of building.

We think that it is a good idea for us to go back to this basic concept of ecclesiastical life in order better to conform our minds to the guidelines which should direct our thoughts and action in this post-conciliar period. We must build the church with Christ and for Christ. Everyone knows that the council has set the church in motion in every field of its activity, and that it has given all of us a sense of renewal, of a new work to be achieved; a sense that fills our hearts with fervor, with hope and with a bit of anxiety over the proper direction and the success of this renewal.[2]

2. Address to General Audience, November 16, 1966.

This is our invitation to continue the journey. The church, with its roots in the past, is also reaching out dynamically toward the future: it guards fidelity as well as hope. Renewal is not restoration of the past. Rather, the church, taking life from the past, wills to go on to meet the Lord, while answering now the needs of the present. Christ was yesterday, is today and will be tomorrow. He is the past, present and future of the church. This is the context in which we wish to live out Vatican II. It leads us from today to tomorrow: from the "already" to the "not yet."

Every work of man, no matter how great, must pay its debt to human weakness. Our gaze can never encompass the whole of the horizon, and we carry the treasures confided to us in vessels of clay. A council itself is stamped with the mark of the time and of the men who made it, and it receives from this stamp its meaning in history and its inevitable limitations. But it also receives its power of movement and its capacity for openness.

THE INITIAL SCHEMAS

Vatican II, we have to admit, was handicapped from the beginning by its own surprise, and by the lacunae in its preparation. "When it comes to councils," John XXIII used to say with a captivating smile, "we are all novices." When we compare preparatory schemas of the council with the definitive texts which were voted upon, we see the long road which had to be traveled in order for the council to be free from theology that was too narrow, too juridic and too defensive.

Let us recall, for example, what was said of the faithful

17

CORESPONSIBILITY IN THE CHURCH

in the first schema of the church, and compare it with what was finally said in chapters II and IV of the constitution *Lumen Gentium.* Or we could compare what was said about church-state relations in the preliminary and final drafts of the *Declaration on Religious Freedom.* Little space was accorded to the young churches in the first schema on the missions, but in the *Decree on the Church's Missionary Activity,* a full chapter was dedicated to them. Allusions to non-Christians were rare and gratuitous in a number of early schemas; and although the subject is still insufficiently treated in revised drafts, nonetheless there are a number of important statements, especially in the *Declaration on the Relationship of the Church to Non-Christian Religions.*

The list could be extended to include all of the council documents. We could point, for instance, to the fundamentalist positions in matters of morality and moral problems as found in the preliminary text of the *Pastoral Constitution on the Church in the Modern World,* and compare it with the finely worded final draft. The first schema on the liturgy was characterized by much timidity, yet there was great openness in the promulgated constitution. The first schema on the source of revelation was polemical, the final draft conciliar and ecumenical. The proposals relating to the formation of the clergy were at first academic, even scholastic, but in the end were pastoral in tone.

Those who lived the council day by day could not help but admire the power of the Holy Spirit guiding the advance of the proceedings. The pace of this advance allowed the fathers of the council to become more reflectively aware of the implications of the council, and helped them to weld a common soul.

There is really nothing new in this review of the history

18

of the preconciliar schemas. When the author was a student at the seminary, his professor of church history recommended the reading of *Concile du Vatican* by F. Mourret. We learned with some surprise that the fathers of Vatican I had not been gentle with the theologians who had prepared their schemas. The Jesuit Ballerini considered the work of his colleagues to have resulted in a *moles indigesta,* an "undigested mass," an *opus de novo conficiendum,* "a work to be done all over again." Bishop Connolly, archbishop of Halifax, demanded that the proposal *de fide catholica* be sent back to the commission *non ad corrigendum, sed ad sepeliendum,* "not for correction, but for burial." This interment was roundly discussed, but happily it finally took place, and the schema was completely redone. Historians of Vatican II will be able to note some parallels.

THE SEARCH FOR UNANIMITY

However paradoxical it might seem, another obstacle to the council's complete actualization was the desire for unanimity. The ideal of rallying all the votes to the texts and decrees proposed constitutes at once the glory and weakness of the council.

This ideal is the glory of a council because the church is a supernatural mystery of communion. A council cannot take on the nature of a parliament, where the majority determines the law for everyone. To indicate this concern for unanimity, the council had foreseen that a proposition would be adopted on the condition that it could gain three-fourths of the votes, and always with the supposition that

19

the pope gave his final assent. As it turned out, in most important matters the voting attained a near unanimity.

The search for unanimity is certainly praiseworthy, but in fact, in the case at Vatican II, it served the interests of the minority. This was not the case of Vatican I, where the situation was just the opposite. In 1870, the bishops who were not favorable to the definition of infallibility hoped to gain advantage for their cause by recalling that a solemn conciliar declaration supposes moral unanimity. A controversy quickly developed, and pamphlets were published on the subject. Those who directed the council saw to it that a study, both historical and theological, was drawn up. This study was put in its final form by the consultor, Sebastian Sanguinetti. It concluded, on the basis of many arguments, that moral unanimity was not necessary. It is true that there is a slight difference between the "search" for moral unanimity and the "necessity" for it, but one can hardly avoid the impression that it is a two-edged sword, and that at Vatican II it weakened the majority.

This unanimity had its own price. During the course of the debates, and because of the introduction of numerous amendments—which ought, on principle, to have been integrated with the rest of the text—it happened that certain passages lost their point and power of impact. It will be the task of historians to disengage the governing and central affirmations of the council from the dross of incidental statements and embellishments. The search for a common denominator did not always do full justice to the authentic mind of the majority. It is not easy to forge a synthesis with elements deriving from different opinions. Sometimes the texts are richer in what they latently imply than in what they affirm on the surface.

20

Within the conciliar texts there are formulas and statements whose role was to provide a balancing or rallying point. At times, they were arrived at like some stair landing on the way to the top. By the very nature of things, and of human interplay, certain accentuations never arrived at their full potential for renewal; but the buds are there now, awaiting the sun's rays. It will be left to men under the impulse of the Holy Spirit to disentangle all the latent forces contained in the conciliar texts, and to bring to light their deep significance. It will be their task also to evaluate all that was said orally at the council itself, or even outside of it, but which nevertheless forms an integrating part of the living context of Vatican II.

THE CONTRIBUTION OF THE EAST

There was also one last weakening factor: the reception, still too timid, which Vatican II accorded to the contributions of the East.

At the beginning, the fundamental and inspiring theology of the council was of an exclusively Latin outlook. The influence of the fathers from the East, nearly always supported by the majority, served, little by little, to correct this monopoly. There was a symbol which ought right away to have led the council fathers to make this correction. The chair of Peter placed at the end of the aula is supported by the Latin fathers St. Augustine and St. Ambrose, and the Greek fathers St. Athanasius and St. John Chrysostom. The symbol was striking; but it was only slowly that its meaning penetrated and became operative in the consciousness of the assembly.

21

Then, the council texts began to speak of the relationship between the mystery of the Holy Trinity and that of the Church, the pneumatic role of the Spirit and that of charisms. A growing conscious recourse was had to the fathers and doctors of the Eastern church. We must continue to advance in this direction. In publishing the oral interventions and written contributions of the Melkite church under the title *The Greek Melkite Church at the Council,* the conciliar fathers from the East wished to point out what appear to them as starting points for the future.

The late Patriarch Maximus IV, said, "There are doors which the Holy Spirit has opened that nevermore will be closed." This Eastern complementarity is a valuable factor for balance and equilibrium, as Cardinal Colombo, archbishop of Milan, has so aptly described:

As the fact of having two eyes allows a man to measure distance and distinguish things, so also, it seems to me, the oriental vision on many problems debated at the council, linked to the vision of the West, enabled me, and enables me today, to understand more deeply the doctrine of Christ.[3]

The East helps us to find once again "the absent half of ourselves." Is it necessary to add that this opening out to the East is by its very nature ecumenical? At least, in saying it, we give expression to all the hope that this opening presages.

The deep and resounding echo set up by the conciliar interventions of the Eastern prelates is not explicable only by the esteem in which the Eastern church is held. For these churches were in fact a symbol of all the non-European churches. Their voice was an appeal to recog-

3. *Bulletin du Patriarcat grec Melkite catholique,* April 30, 1967, p. 9.

nize the fact that the sister churches of Asia, Africa and Latin America are equally capable, as are the churches of Europe, to assume their own character and their own proper structure. Even more profoundly, it was sensed that this recognition of diversity could have important repercussions on the day when the question of the Anglican and other Christian churches came to the fore. All of this was already at work in the reception given to the fathers from the East, and even now the relations between Rome and Constantinople manifest its fruit.

The Present Moment

If we turn our attention from future prospects and look at the actual situation, we must recognize that the church lives right now in troubled times. For some, Vatican II is nothing more than a parenthetical event; while for others, it is an event already lost in history: they are concentrating on the future.

While some enter but little or not at all into the conciliar renewal, others give themselves up to pitiless criticism of what they call the ecclesiastical "system." It even happens that this criticism, under pretext of pruning dead branches, puts the ax to the root of the tree, so that faith in the supernatural reality of the church seems compromised.

The first group, in order to save what they deem essential, are opposed to any pruning. As they defend the faith they also defend theological and disciplinary immobility; and they strive to maintain usages, customs and methods which are already out of date. They never hesitate to de-

23

nounce any excesses from a position safe in the fortress with all the drawbridges up.

The second group make their voice heard in numberless books, articles, newspapers and interviews. They promote radical revision of institutions and methods at the risk of shattering dogmas, moral principles and liturgy. The so-called crisis of the "third man" has many ramifications. This "third man" is one who frees himself from objective values, such as dogma, law and institutions, appealing all the while to the gospel.

We live in a time of imbalance and of searching, in which it is easy to succumb to the temptation of assuming an exclusive position either for the past as it was, or for a future without roots in the past. But we cannot accept such a dilemma. The church is not itself if it is not at one and the same time past, present and future. In the church, the past is always operative, and the future is already present. In it, tradition is perpetual renewal, and growth, at its deepest level, is a real continuity. The past is mother earth to the future; a church which lacked continuity with tradition would no longer be the church of Christ.

The church's reality is like that of the eucharist. These two mysteries are deeply related; for if the church makes the eucharist it is also true that the eucharist makes the church. But the eucharist is at one and the same time a memorial of the past, a present actualization of that unique sacrifice offered once for all, and an anticipation of the future resurrection: memorial, actuality and prophecy.

The eucharist remains the same throughout the ages. Since Holy Thursday evening, it gives unchangeable expression to itself, in the same sacred words which it repeats in memory of the Master until he comes.

24

And yet what variety there has been in the accidentals over the centuries! The eucharist has been celebrated in the most diverse liturgies. It has expressed itself in Aramaic, in Greek, Latin, Slavonic, Coptic and Chaldean, and at the present time it speaks all languages. It has sung Gregorian chant and polyphony, and now it sings the music of all the people it meets, making itself all things to all men. It has prayed in the balanced, classical phrases of Rome, and has taken into its heart the lyricism and exuberance of the East. Now, it is aware of the need to express itself according to the mind of modern man.

Not only have language and modes of expression varied over the ages, but the Upper Room has been reproduced in many varied circumstances: on the altar of a martyr in the catacombs, in the great villa of a patrician convert, in the basilicas of Constantine, in the Roman churches, in the cathedrals, both Gothic and Baroque, and today in the essential simplicity of our modern churches. It is always the same eucharist being expressed through a liturgy which is faithful to the past and open to the present.

Something analogous takes place within the heart of the church in regard to theological and pastoral development. To those Christians who are upset and distracted by questioning and new research, we would say that faith is both certitude and continual quest. It is normal, and in itself quite healthy, that theologians periodically revise the formulas in which our dogma and beliefs are expressed.

We tend to think of the faith as a body of truths fixed in their expression which are to be handed on like ingots of gold in a treasure coffer. But faith is life and the source of life; whatever is alive is bound to grow, and to grow continually: there lies the heart of the problem.

25

Faith is like an ancient oak tree. Its roots are plunged in the nourishing soil of the church's tradition. If the sap is to rise and give life to the tree, it must be surrounded by a protective bark which is formed slowly by the work of successive generations. The bark is not the sap, yet it derives its nourishment therefrom. They are intimately connected: what impinges on the outside of the tree has effects within.

The life-giving sap of the faith-tree is the living word of God as he reveals himself. Our dogmatic and theological formulas serve to protect and contain this sap. They derive their nourishment from within. They are "spirit and life," but they are also, in part, conditioned by their habitat and surrounding climate.

It rarely happens that a truth is defined in itself and for itself. Generally, in the course of history, a truth is expressed because of some denial, some exclusive concentration, some heresy which arises. And thus, succeeding generations must exercise constant care that this defined truth receive the proper complementarity and harmony it needs in order to remain fully faithful to itself.

In his discourse which opened Vatican II, John XXIII traced out the history of these legitimate definitions, while also indicating the distinction between the substance of the faith and its modes of expression.

But from the renewed, serene, and tranquil adherence to all the teaching of the Church in its entirety and preciseness, as it still shines forth in the Acts of the Council of Trent and First Vatican Council, the Christian, Catholic, and apostolic spirit of the whole world expects a step forward toward a doctrinal penetration and a formation of consciousness in faithful and perfect conformity to the authentic doctrine, which, however, should be studied and expounded through the methods of research and through the

26

literary forms of modern thought. The substance of the ancient doctrine of the deposit of faith is one thing, and the way in which it is presented is another. And it is the latter that must be taken into great consideration with patience if necessary, everything being measured in the forms and proportions of a magisterium which is predominantly pastoral in character.

Pope Paul VI was even more precise. Speaking to theologians, he said:

For we are fully convinced that bishops and priests cannot worthily carry out their mission of enlightening and saving the modern world if they are not in a position to present, defend and illustrate the truths of divine faith with ideas and words that are more understandable to minds trained in present-day philosophical and scientific learning.[4]

If this way of envisaging a problem is extended to all of Christian doctrine, the significance of such an orientation is clearly seen. The reason why new concepts and new formulations must always be sought is that revealed reality is a mystery, and will remain such eternally. The closer we come to the heart of a mystery the less equipped we are to express its content, and the more legitimate becomes the search for more adequate formulations. At the opening of the second session of the council, on September 29, 1963, Paul VI, speaking of the mystery of the church, gave clear expression to this fact when he said:

It is the nature of the human mind to advance in thought and learning. From the apprehension of empirical truths it rises to a higher, more scientific understanding of those truths which, in turn,

4. Address of Paul VI to the Participants in the Symposium on Original Sin, July 11, 1966.

by a logical process of deduction, give rise to the knowledge of
further truths. And when the mind is confronted with a complex
reality, yet one which is possessed of primary certitude, it pauses
to consider the various aspects of this truth, one after another. We
thus have that development in the activity of the inquiring mind to
which history bears constant witness.

And we are convinced that the time has now come for a more
thorough investigation into the truth which concerns the church.
This truth must be subjected to a more intensive examination, and
given formulation—not, perhaps, as a solemn, dogmatic pronounce-
ment, but certainly in declarations expressing in a clearer and
more authoritative form the Church's teaching about herself.

The church's self-awareness increases with her unswerving adherence to the thought and utterances of Christ, her reverence for
the proven precepts of sacred tradition, and her response to the
inner guidance of the Holy Spirit. It is he who now seems to be
urging the Church to make every effort to gain the recognition of
all men for what she is.

All the indications lead us to believe that in this council the
truth-giving Spirit will shed a brighter radiance over the sacred
ranks of the teaching church, and inspire a clearer doctrine regarding the church's nature.

Continual adaptation has a place in the church so long
as we do not abuse the word "adaptation" and give to it a
superficial meaning. We abuse the word when we take it to
mean a thoughtless conformity to the tastes and fads of the
day, an arbitrary selection among the truths of the faith:
this is not adaptation but corruption. But the word cannot
refer merely to surface realities: continual adaptation is not
merely a periodic readjustment of objective formulations
which never touches the heart of things.

The church must always seek dialogue between its faith
and a world which is developing and constantly posing new
problems as it approaches new thresholds of knowledge.

28

This means that the church must ever penetrate more deeply the content of its own faith.

Pope Paul VI expressed this confrontation in his allocution to the pilgrims from Brescia:

> How can we transmit in new forms the heritage of antiquity and of the recent past, when no one can deny that our society is undergoing a radical transformation, and that thought, culture, manner of life, economics, social life and even the religious feeling and its expressions, are in a state of total evolution? How can we treat the heritage of the past in the perspective of today and tomorrow?

The church must imitate the wise householder of the gospel, and take from her treasure both new things and old. This kind of renewal may disturb those who wish for ready-made solutions, eternal formulations, easy and quick answers for problems that arise; but this cannot be helped.

Each generation must take up the pilgrim's staff and continue the search, in order to make and renew the dialogue with the world around it. We are committed to exploring continually the riches of revelation. It will be a rare joy to be able at the end of our pilgrimage to repeat these words of the poet:

> *We shall not cease from exploration*
> *and the end of all our exploring*
> *will be to arrive where we started*
> *and know the place for the first time.*[5]

Coresponsibility, the Central Idea of Vatican II

Certainly Vatican II had its limitations; it neither approached nor resolved all problems. Nevertheless, we must recognize

5. T. S. Eliot, *Four Quartets*, "Little Gidding" (Part V).

that it has opened upon immense horizons. It has sown, in the field of the church, seeds which give promise of maturity at harvest time. If we were to be asked what we consider to be that seed of life deriving from the council which is most fruitful in pastoral consequences, we would answer without any hesitation: it is the rediscovery of the people of God as a whole, as a single reality; and then by way of consequence, the coresponsibility thus implied for every member of the church.

In presenting the church as the people of God, the council immediately took a stand, more fundamental than the organic and functional distinction between hierarchy and laity, and considered that which is common to all—baptism. "One Lord, one faith, one baptism," all of a sudden this affirmation of scripture assumed its full importance. It is the same baptism which makes all Christians children of God, brothers in Christ, sanctified by the Holy Spirit.

Whether they be members of the hierarchy or not, all Christians are first and foremost "the faithful" in the deepest meaning of this word, that is, "the believers." We can never meditate enough on the baptismal foundation of the church, this primal mystery of Christian existence, which unites in one decisive act the acceptance of the Lord, the profession of the gospel, the purification from sin, the active presence of the Spirit, and entrance into the community of the faithful.

The sacrament of baptism is the gateway to Christian life. The other sacraments suppose that we have already "entered." Their perspective is different. Baptism is the root of all Christian life, and of all religious life, be it structured or not. It is that point from which all vocations,

30

functions and charisms derive their life. In the church of God, this fundamental equality of all is the primary fact. There is no superbaptism, there are no castes, no privileges (Gal. 3, 28).

We must always be aware of these fundamental truths, for they are essential to the life of the church, and govern all our choices and attitudes. For too long a time and too frequently, we have confused the terms "layman" and "faithful." The pope or a bishop or priest is not a layman, but he is one of the faithful by the very fact that he is baptized and a Christian.

The greatest day in the life of a pope is not that of his election or coronation, but the day on which he receives that which the Greek fathers call the holy and unbreakable seal of baptismal regeneration. His first duty, like that of all of us, is to live the Christian life in obedience to the gospel. His own proper mission derives from this duty.

Some theologies of the laity have attributed to the layman as such that which, in fact, pertains to him as one of the faithful. Some authors speak of the layman's share in the royal, priestly, prophetic and apostolic functions of the church. They are, in fact, speaking of that share in these realities which the faithful as such have, insofar as they are baptized, confirmed and participate in the liturgy.

This is a very important point. Whatever pertains to the duties of the faithful simply as such, continues to be valid for a priest after his ordination, or for a religious after his profession. This fact runs the risk of being forgotten when, in the effort to define the layman as such, we are inclined to set him over and against the priest and religious. From this derives a tendency to refuse to the priest or religious that which is considered proper to the layman.

31

If we except those things which are written about the spirituality of marriage, and the duties inherent in various secular vocations, nearly everything that has been written on the theology of the laity is valid also for men and women religious. For, as a matter of fact, what is said there is but a healthy theology of the Christian life as such.

The decision to include within the *Constitution on the Church* a chapter on the people of God sanctioned the desire of the council to derive all that ought to be said concerning the mission, functions and tasks of the faithful from the "common" or universal Christian condition. The secondary discussions which can legitimately exist in regard to this subject ought never cause us to lose sight of the fundamental meaning of the whole of this chapter.

This primacy of baptism entails as an immediate corollary the primacy of community. Each one must live and insert his personal responsibility in and with that of all the other faithful. Vatican II asks us to accept all the consequences of the coresponsibility of Christians at every level.

It is possible to differentiate individuals and groups within the people of God on the basis of divinely conferred function or charism, and to discuss coresponsibility in terms of these groups. But, in regard to all these distinctions, we must bear in mind the fundamental principle enunciated by St. Paul, that all these gifts conspire toward the building up of the "perfect man" (Eph. 4, 13). This principle is applied to the distinction between laity and hierarchy, and is beautifully expressed in the *Constitution on the Church* when it says, "For the distinction which the Lord made between the sacred ministers and the rest of the people of God entails a unifying purpose, since pastors and the other

32

faithful are bound to each other by a mutual need" (art. 32).

Thus in our discussion of coresponsibility we will treat not only of how the people of God as a whole must answer the call of the Lord as expressed in the needs of our time, but also how this coresponsibility is operative in and between the various groups established on the basis of function or charism within the church. There is

the coresponsibility of the papacy
the coresponsibility of bishops
the coresponsibility of priests
the coresponsibility of theologians
the coresponsibility of deacons
the coresponsibility of religious
the coresponsibility of laymen.

At every one of these levels, Vatican II desires more organic collaboration. It gave birth to institutions which will henceforth form a part of the very life of the church, and which, enlivened by the Spirit of the council, will produce their fruit in the years to come.

But we wish to be well understood. We are not speaking exclusively, or even primarily, of organized collaboration for mere practical pastoral efficiency, but rather of a co-operation which is the corollary and manifestation of the church's deepest nature.

Jerome Hamer has written a book whose title, *The Church is a Communion,* is at once an invitation and an appeal. Pastoral activity can and must derive its vital movement from this central dogmatic basis. But before studying the exigencies which coresponsibility demands at every level, we should first become aware of those common goals which must be achieved by our common effort.

33

Thus there is a preliminary question which we should consider at the outset of our reflections: what are the Church's great needs at the moment? What realities in the Church's life experience must be faced and answered by all of us together? "Lord," St. Paul said as he lay on the road to Damascus, "what do you wish me to do?" The modern church, on its way toward its third millennium, can have no other prayer than this. Such an attitude determines its availability, its involvement, its very reason for being.

II.

The Demands
of Our Time

Every era has its vocation, every age answers to an idea and a desire of the Lord. The time in which we live is the place where we meet the "today of God." Christ has taught us to have on our lips and in our hearts the prayer, "Your will be done on earth . . ." We pray that God's will be done on this earth, our earth, the globe on which we walk, the earth of our time and generation. As we listen to what our age demands of us and place ourselves at its service, we give substance to this desire expressed by the Lord's prayer.

God is at one and the same time eternal and infinitely real; or as Péguy says, he is "both youthful and eternal."

What then is the particular vocation of our time? It seems to me that we can find it in certain words of the gospel which shed light on the whole of church history with new urgency and breadth. There is first of all the command of the Master to his disciples: "Go preach the gospel to every creature . . . and behold I am with you until the end of ages." This is a missionary mandate.

But there is one reality absolutely necessary for the fulfillment of this mission: "Father, may they be one in us, as you are in me and I am in you, so that the world may believe it was you who sent me" (Jn. 17, 21). The unity of Christians among themselves is of primary importance. It is the prelude to any acceptance of, or confidence in, the gospel message. The ecumenical summons being issued today by the Spirit of the Lord to all those who invoke his name is one of the signs of our times. We must be able to receive and be willing to understand it. Our first duty is to direct our energies toward a restoration of a visible unity whose source is the intimate unity of the Trinity. Thus the duty of ecumenical effort and that of missionary activity are mutually related. Our inner coresponsibility is our first acceptance of the duty of coresponsibility with all men of good will.

We are to be "one . . . so that the world may believe." This implies, then, a presence to the world at an ever deeper level, an insertion into this modern world, described by Pope Paul VI as "magnificent and complex, terrible and tormented." And thus the three great demands of our time stand out in bold relief: the call to ecumenism, the call to be missionary, and the call to be present to the world.

Ecumenical Urgency

The council did not hesitate to say that the ecumenical movement bears the obvious stamp of the Holy Spirit. The conciliar decree on ecumenism, and the directives determining its practical application, open up possibilities that are rich with promise.

From now on, there is a new climate of rediscovered brotherhood. Obviously, this climate has not done away with real doctrinal differences. There are some who seem to resign themselves to this situation, as though it had to be permanent. "The glaciers may melt but the Alps will remain." We cannot share this pessimistic view. Even now men are digging into the sides of the mountain, challenging its resistance and preparing for tunnels.

We await the hour of full communion, and in order to hasten it we have learned once again to pray together. We cherish the memory of that prayer in common, presided over by Paul VI at the end of the council, and of the meeting between Patriarch Athenagoras and Pope Paul at the end of the synod. And now we have agreed upon a common text for the "Our Father"; this is at once a symbol and a cause for hope.

Then again, we have sketched some rough outlines for concerted action. In particular, we have begun to join our efforts in the service of the people of developing countries. For we know that we must meet this major social problem of our time together. An economist of world-wide reputation, Barbara Ward, has already well described this ecumenical effort in the service of the "third world."

This point is of immense importance. The ecumenical movement has raised such hopes and expectations that any future failure to work together, as Christians, would breed a corresponding disillusion. Yet in specifically doctrinal matters, progress is likely to be slow and the scope, though wide, possibly more limited than the more ardent spirits hope. Nor is it, in general, a matter for lay leadership.

But in the field of the kinds of social action needed to set the wealth of the West working in a new effort to mitigate world poverty—and domestic poverty, too, for that matter—the possibilities of action are very wide indeed and could become the main field of ecumenical action over the next four or five decades during which many of the crucial changes in the developing world will be taking place.

Sustained by prayer and the fraternal service of others, we cherish the desire to draw closer to one another in matters of doctrine. The many dialogues already begun contain and express this power of attraction. The search for full communion in faith is at the heart of any authentic ecumenism, and is as far removed as possible from a common pragmatism. The Lord prayed that his own consecrate themselves in the truth. We must adhere first of all to this intention of the Lord, if we wish to be faithful to all he expects of us. No diplomatic compromise is possible in matters which are not at our free disposition. But there is room for long and patient efforts in order to clarify dogmatic formulas which can always be rendered more precisely, and manifest their wealth of meaning more fully.

THE PAPAL PRIMACY

We all know that the great obstacles that separate us from our non-Catholic brothers are the dogmas of papal primacy and infallibility. In an allocution to the members of the Secretariat for Promoting Christian Unity, Pope Paul VI recognized this obstacle himself, when he said:

We know full well that the papacy is undoubtedly the most serious obstacle on the ecumenical road. What are we to say? Should we appeal once again to the evidence that validates our mission? Should we try once again to present in precise terms what it purports to be: the necessary principle of truth, charity and unity? Should we show once again that it is a pastoral charge of direction, service and brotherhood which does not challenge the freedom or dignity of anyone who has a legitimate problem in the church of God, but which rather protects the rights of all and only claims the obedience called for among children in the same family? It is not easy for us to plead our own cause.[1]

Here too, then, we have a new climate, which can be symbolized by two images: that of John XXIII receiving the observers at the council, and Paul VI on pilgrimage to Jerusalem and Constantinople. We begin to perceive at the level of concrete reality what a primacy of service and love can be.

After Vatican I, the papacy appeared to the non-Catholic world as an absolute monarchy, incompatible with any kind of collegiality. Men like Bismarck and Gladstone gave voice to this impression. But the very fact that John XXIII convoked a council shows quite clearly that collegiality is more than a word; and the *Constitution on the Church* has expressed its reality and significance. Theologians will have to locate the dogma of papal primacy more precisely within the context of collegiality, showing especially, as we have just said, that the primacy should be understood first of all as a service. This context of the papacy will, we hope, allow all Christians to enter more deeply into an understanding of the dogma.

But there is nothing that will free the papacy more completely from all suspicion of absolutism and authoritarianism than the application in daily life of the doctrinal

1. Allocution of April 28, 1967.

39

principle of "primacy of service." This will be more effective than doctrinal discussion.

Michael Ramsey, primate of the Anglican church, expresses the same opinion when speaking of the famous meetings at Malines, where papers were presented attempting to define the relationships between the episcopacy and the papacy. He writes:

> For a primacy should depend upon and express the organic authority of the Body; and the discovery of its precise functions will come not by discussion of the Petrine claims in isolation but by the recovery everywhere of the Body's life, with its Bishops, presbyters and people. In this Body Peter will find his due place, and ultimate reunion is hastened not by the pursuit of "the Papal controversy" but by the quiet growth of the organic life of every part of Christendom.[2]

In our opinion, theological research is indispensable, but it is in the very experience of the church that primacy must be lived out; and this is of the greatest importance. This experience will be the fruit of a coresponsibility fully accepted and lived by the bishops individually, and by the episcopal conferences, as well as by the whole Christian community. Arguments in the abstract about hypothetical conflict of power, and efforts at increasing juridical precisions, will not hasten the time of deep mutual understanding.

The council was an important landmark on the road toward doctrinal clarification. The intimate life of the church and the ecumenical dialogue itself cannot but experience the consequences of this important step.

2. M. Ramsey, *The Gospel and the Church,* London, 1956, p. 228.

PAPAL INFALLIBILITY

What is true of papal primacy is also true of papal infallibility. It receives new light when placed in the context and perspective of the whole church.

In recalling that "The body of the faithful as a whole, anointed as they are by the Holy One, cannot err in matters of belief" the *Constitution on the Church* (art. 12) helps to situate better the role of episcopal inerrancy and papal infallibility in the exercise of their highest teaching office. It is the Lord who is the source of the indefectibility of his whole church. The hierarchical ministry of the gospel truth is a service to the whole community.

We hope that the time is coming when this ecclesial perspective will be more accentuated in Catholic theology, so that other Christians will be led for their part to rethink and perhaps revise their attitude toward papal infallibility.

It is undeniable that the definition of infallibility has been so stressed in Catholic ecclesiology since 1870, that the infallibility of the church itself, so obvious to all that no one thought it necessary to define it, was overshadowed and even neglected. But the inerrancy of the pope speaking *ex cathedra* was defined in reference to the infallibility of the church. The exercise of this "prerogative" is conditioned by the various limits established by the definition itself.

Before the final vote, Bishop Gasser, secretary for the Commission of the Faith at Vatican I, made this very significant declaration:

Absolute infallibility belongs to God alone, who is the first and essential Truth, and who can never in any way be mistaken or

41

led into error. Every other infallibility by the very fact that it is conferred for a well-defined goal has its limits and conditions. And so it is with the infallibility of the Roman pontiff.[3]

Thus to speak of infallibility is constantly to return above all to the promise of the Lord, "I am with you until the end of ages." This divine assistance and protection is always present. The definition of Vatican I affirms that infallibility is exercised with certitude and efficacy when the Roman pontiff speaks *ex cathedra,* and only when he speaks *ex cathedra.* This is so true that in his authoritative discourse, which is of such great importance for the understanding of the definition, Bishop Gasser could say that the statement "the pope is infallible" is too imprecise. Rather, "the pope is only infallible when, in a solemn judgment, he defines for the universal church a question of faith or morals."[4]

Already at the First Vatican Council the most enthusiastic defenders of papal infallibility refrained from proposing a "separate" infallibility. They admitted that the pope is never separated from his church, and that they too did not wish a "beheading of Peter."[5] For, they explained, it is one thing to affirm that in certain well-defined circumstances the Roman pontiff is able personally to define a truth, and it is another thing to think that at the moment when he thus exercises his supreme dogmatic judgment the pope is actually separated from the church.[6]

Bishop Gasser would explain later that the pope is joined to the church in many ways. He is united to it, first of all,

3. Mansi, *Amplissima Collectio Conciliorum,* T. 52, col. 1214.
4. *Ibid.,* 52, 1213.
5. *Ibid.,* 52, 37.
6. *Ibid.,* 52, 36.

THE DEMANDS OF OUR TIME

because the head is never separated from the body, and the building cannot stand without its foundation.[7]

He is also united by the very fact that the statements to be made in matters of doctrine arise first at a local or regional level, and only arrive at the level of the pope last of all.

A definition is justified, first of all, when there appear in some part of the church, scandals regarding the faith, disagreements, or heresies, which the leaders of the church, taken individually, or even assembled in provincial council, are not able to correct, and thus find themselves forced to refer the matter to the apostolic see.[8]

Certainly the "first of all" in Bishop Gasser's address leaves the door open to exceptions, but nevertheless it indicates the "normal" line to be followed.

When he pronounces a definition, the Roman pontiff has the moral obligation to be informed about the truth in question. And in this regard, once again, the normal vehicle of information is the episcopacy, and at their own level, the theologians. Thus Bishop Gasser goes on to say,

We do not exclude at all the cooperation of the church; for the infallibility of the Roman pontiff is given to him, not by way of inspiration or revelation, but by way of divine assistance. That is why the pope in exercising his responsibility, according to the gravity of the problems, must use adequate means to investigate the truth as it deserves, and to state it correctly. These means are the councils and also the advice of bishops, the cardinals, the theologians, etc.[9]

There is a question here of those instances, actually quite rare, when the pope would be obliged to pronounce a

7. *Ibid.,* 52, 1213.
8. *Ibid.*
9. *Ibid.*

43

definition alone, in virtue of the promise given by Christ to Peter and his successors. And, since the pope can discover the faith of the church in other ways, one could conclude that it is not "absolutely" necessary that the pope gain his information from among the episcopacy.

Sometimes the meaning of the text of Vatican I has been overstressed and it was forgotten that what was denied there was the strict and absolute juridical necessity of consulting the bishops. Normally, it is from among the bishops first of all that the sovereign pontiff receives his information in those rare instances when he considers himself obliged to make a definition.

In fact, since there is question of a definition, the faith is at issue, and thus the ordinary teaching authority of the bishop is involved. Once again, in the words of Bishop Gasser, "The unanimous approval expressed by the actual preaching of the whole of the church's magisterium, united with its head, is also the rule of faith for pontifical definitions."[10]

Briefly, whatever be the manner in which the pope informs himself, he must remain in perfect communion with the faith of the whole church. As Cardinal Dechamps wrote a short time after Vatican I, "Some type of consensus or actual accord in the faith is absolutely indispensable to infallibility."[11]

It is well known that Protestants do not like the term "infallibility." Actually, this term came into theology during the 14th century; one could also use the terms "inde-

10. *Ibid.,* 52, 1216.
11. Unpublished response of Cardinal Dechamps to Bishop Kettler; cf. *Revue des sciences philosophiques et théologiques* (1935), pp. 296–299.

THE DEMANDS OF OUR TIME

fectibility in matters of faith," "immunity from error," or "inerrancy." In ancient times, one spoke rather of truth, as does the bible. And perhaps we should return to this manner of expressing ourselves in order to facilitate a deeper mutual understanding.

THE HOLY SPIRIT AND CONVERGING TENDENCIES

As the ecumenical dialogue continues, we are able to discern converging tendencies, movements of the Spirit, which lead toward the unity of all Christians. Truths and values which at one time seemed to cancel each other out now present themselves as complementary.

Ancient antinomies are tending to resolve themselves: tradition or scripture, hierarchy or priesthood of the faithful, papacy or collegiality. There are many examples of similar efforts to go beyond the impasse of a false dualism and to achieve harmonic unity.

Vatican II says again and again, that all hierarchy is service to the people of God, and insists upon the priestly and charismatic role of the faithful. At the same time, various studies emanating from the reform churches show that Luther was attacking the hierarchy of his time, not the hierarchical principle itself.[12]

The council put great stress on episcopal collegiality, and upon respect for particular churches; though we perceive at the same time in many places outside of Rome a certain nostalgia for unity.

In the Protestant world we see the monks of Taizé de-

12. Cf. H. Lieberg, *Amt und Ordination bei Luther und Melanchthon*, Göttingen, 1962.

45

fending the real presence in the eucharist, the relevance of monasticism, the value of celibacy for the kingdom of God, and honoring Mary under the title of Mother of the Lord. A very important Protestant work examines the Marian piety of the early reformers, and Cardinal Martin wrote the preface for the new edition of Martin Luther's commentary on the *Magnificat*.

Catholics are insisting more on the transcendent holiness of God and the complete gratuity of his gift of grace, while Protestants are tending to integrate better the concept of "good works" and the witness of faith.

Catholics are insisting on the necessity of placing sacramental rites within the context of the life of faith, while at the same time the reformers are taking another look at the question of ministry and its necessary and constitutive role within the church.

Catholics are reaffirming the importance of episcopal collegiality and its connection with the papacy, and the Orthodox and Anglicans and other "episcopal" churches are calling to mind that antiquity considered the first apostolic see, Rome, as the ultimate arbiter and center of ecclesiastical communion. We also see Protestant churches accepting the necessity for authority in the church in order that certain reforms be effected, and in so doing they are thus moving toward some kind of episcopal structure.

In brief, we see a tendency to replace opposing dilemmas by a unifying synthesis with all the enrichment that this implies for a greater realization and manifestation of true catholicity.[13]

Not so long ago, none of these tendencies was even thought of. They witness to the fact that, over and above

13. Cf. *Decree on Ecumenism*, art. 4.

those things which still divide us, there is an ever growing concern for our common task. Our generation has seen effected within itself a spiritual revolution launched by the Spirit.

We once asked an Orthodox friend, who was an observer at the council, what he thought was the principal obstacle to union. He said to me, "The fact that we haven't been speaking for nine centuries." Today, dialogue has begun again, hearts are opening out to hope. The Holy Spirit will confirm and strengthen that which he has begun.

Missionary Urgency

"May they be one that the world may believe." These words of the Master sound the keynote of the twofold obligation: to be ecumenical and to be missionary.

In a way exceeding any of its predecessors, Vatican II proclaimed the duty of going out to all men, even to the ends of the earth. We do not have to go too far back in history to find an age where the equation "a Christian = an apostle" was considered a paradox. It was not understood that a Christian is not truly a Christian till he is a "Christianizer"; that he has not truly received the gospel until he understands and accepts the responsibility to preach it.

As we were preparing our book *The Gospel to Every Creature,* we searched through religious literature trying to find texts which treated of the apostolic and missionary duty of every baptized Christian, but we had great difficulty in finding any. In a review of the book, we were criticized for maintaining as a fundamental text, "Go out into the

47

whole world and proclaim the good news to all creation"
(Mk. 16, 17), and for extending to every Christian an
invitation, or an order, which concerned only the apostles.
However, there is neither a lack of texts nor a difficulty in
applying them, if we prescind from the internal distinction
within the church, and raise the issue to the level of the
church as a whole. The church, as such, is missionary by
essence and definition. It is the church as the people of God
which is entrusted, in coresponsibility, with the duty of
evangelizing the world. The council said this first of all in
the *Constitution on the Church.* Then, during the period
between sessions, this concept matured and the council
said it again with greater force and precision in the *Decree
on the Church's Missionary Activity.* Let us listen to the
council expressing itself in these two series of texts:

> The pilgrim church is missionary by her very nature. For it is
> from the mission of the Son and the mission of the Holy Spirit
> that she takes her origin, in accordance with the decree of God
> the Father (*Decree,* art. 2).

The primary and most important task of this mission is
to proclaim the good news to all men:

> The church has been divinely sent to all nations that she might
> be "the universal sacrament of salvation" (*Constitution,* art. 48).
> Acting out of the innermost requirements of her own catholicity
> and in obedience to her Founder's mandate, she strives to proclaim
> the gospel to all men (*Decree,* Preface).

> The church has received from the apostles this solemn mandate
> of Christ to proclaim the saving truth even to the ends of the earth.
> Hence she makes the words of the apostle her own: "Woe to me,
> if I do not preach the gospel," (1 Cor. 9, 16), and continues un-

48

ceasingly to send heralds of the gospel until such a time as the infant churches are fully established and can themselves carry on the work of evangelizing (*Constitution*, art. 17).

Since the whole church is missionary, and the work of evangelization is a basic duty of the people of God, this sacred synod summons all to a deep interior renewal. Thus, from a vivid awareness of their own responsibility for spreading the gospel, they will do their share in missionary work among the nations (*Decree*, art. 35).

The obligation of spreading the faith is imposed on every disciple of Christ, according to his ability (*Constitution*, art. 17).

Thus the council completely confirmed what Albert Dondeyne had written a few years earlier:

The Church is by its essence a missionary community. It continues and extends the apostolic community founded by Christ to proclaim the message. It springs from the word of God, and is at the service of that word. In its capacity as the new Israel, it assumes and renews the mission of the chosen people in regard to the salvation of the world. The biblical concept of election is not synonymous with lack of concern. Election cannot be separated from the notions of mission and ministry. Divine election, while it creates a particularly close relationship to God, implies the notion of vocation or call, and consequently, that of responsibility before God. Through baptism and faith, the Christian becomes a member of the apostolic community. He enters into God's intentions for the world. He is called to open himself out to God's saving will for sinful humanity, and that is why from now on his prayer will be "May your kingdom come, may your will be done . . ." This means that belonging to the church of Christ is at once a grace and a responsibility: it is the duty of every Christian to collaborate in the "building up" of the church, in both senses of the word "edify."[14]

14. "Fondements théologiques du laïcat missionaire," *Echanges* (June 1964), pp. 10–11.

49

A CRISIS IN THE CONCEPT OF MISSION

There is light in this doctrine of the council, but we must admit that the climate in the post-conciliar period is far from corresponding to its ideals. From every side, and for the most different reasons, the very concept of mission is under heavy fire in the church today.

We would list as a general cause that spirit of exclusive and horizontal humanism which, even among Christians, is leading them to minimize the sense of God and of his transcendence, and the sense of sin and redemption. There is such an enthusiasm for temporal values that the work of evangelization is esteemed but little—it seems to be a stranger to what is human, to be useless and too spiritual. Such an outlook is unable to understand that true evangelization contains within itself not only a religious dimension but a social and temporal dimension as well.

Then there are some particular reasons which militate against the missionary concept, or at least render it a disservice. There is first and foremost an ever growing fear of encroaching upon liberty of conscience, a liberty accentuated by the council itself. Then there is, too, the realization, more vivid today but always known, that there are elements of truth, elements of the gospel, scattered throughout all religions. The success realized by the concept of dialogue has served in its own way to overshadow evangelization. It could actually appear that the more one dialogues the less one evangelizes. And in our culture, which is becoming more and more characterized by dialogue, the age of evangelization seems to have passed. But we cannot accept this kind of reasoning.

50

No doubt, Catholics find themselves in contact with men of more refined culture and with people more aware of the inherent value of their own religion. Thus a certain rather romantic idea of what it means to preach the gospel is rapidly disappearing. Those who wish to announce the Christian message find themselves obliged to adopt a manner of acting more in keeping with adults. But to lay aside a romantic kind of gospel preaching does not mean that we ought to abandon evangelization completely.

It is a natural instinct when one meets an adult to engage in a dialogue suitable to his person. But to dialogue is not the same as to sink the ship one stands on. It implies, of course, a certain mutual exchange, and means that the Catholic does not present himself to other believers as somebody "having it all" talking to those who have nothing. But at the same time, true dialogue demands that its participants present their own proper belief precisely and seriously, and with real foundations. Such a presentation is usually more demanding and reflective than that engaged in with someone who still has everything to learn. A Catholic has to make an effort so that his interlocutor understands Catholicism as exactly as possible. What follows, the response to this call and adherence to it, is left to the grace of the Lord. And is not this a way in which the church usually presents itself when it announces the Christian message to adults in those places where it is already established?

We say "usually." For if, in fact, our age is one characterized more and more by dialogue, and the method of ecumenical dialogue seems to be more and more called for, it is still true that in Christian countries the work of reconciliation—we used to say conversion—still remains fundamental. The *Decree on Ecumenism* makes the following

51

observation: "It is evident that the work of preparing and reconciling those individuals who wish for full catholic communion is of its nature distinct from ecumenical action. But there is no opposition between the two, since both proceed from the wondrous providence of God" (art. 4).

The explanation of this text is quite simple. It is possible, and even normal, that certain people are called by divine grace actually to become "Roman Catholics." Thus it is necessary that for these people the Church create or maintain structures whose goal is "to prepare" directly for reconciliation. But a manner of presentation which is possible among Christians would seem to assume a much more important role when placed in a non-Christian context. To that degree it is fitting that the church think in terms of suitable structures which can "prepare" the approach to Catholicism, thus maintaining some direct evangelical activity. Here again, one must present Catholicism in an adult or ecumenical way; and such a presentation pertains to an authentic preaching of the gospel.

THE DUTY OF SPEAKING

There are those who tend to oversimplify things and see in the conciliar *Declaration on Religious Freedom* such a demand for respect of liberty of conscience that it would reduce all missionaries to silence. It would be the end of direct apostolic action.

Of course, the act of faith is a free act, and can tolerate no constraint. The history of the church is not without errors and deficiencies in this regard, and we must admit it. But concern to eliminate coercion is not identical with silence. Let the missionary approach the unbeliever with great respect for liberty of conscience, let him approach with tact; but let him also speak.

It is this very respect for another that urges us to speak to him. To make no effort to pass on the word of God would result in a lack of esteem for that word, and a lack of interest in those to whom it is addressed as a message of life and salvation. Vatican II in no way renders direct missionary activity out of date; it is not the patron of witnesses whom respect has rendered mute. We have to avoid this temptation to silence, and exorcise the "dumb spirits."

To be a missionary will always be a duty inspired by love for men, but first and foremost it must be inspired by love for God. The Christian mission derives its origin and its urgency from God. It is God who wishes to communicate himself, and each of us is chosen to aid in the preparation of this meeting between God and man.

God's love is a desire for free and total communion. He desires this impatiently, for this kind of impatience is inherent in any love which wishes to give itself. We say so easily that God is patient. There are many Christians who are content in the faith of this so-called patience of God, and abstain from any apostolate. God is patient because we force him to be. He is burning to give himself. So long as the chosen people made light of the covenant which he offered them, God never ceased to complain of their reluctance. Throughout all of scripture he gives free rein to his expressions of impatience, which is one aspect of his love.

We must become aware of the living relevance of our Lord's words, "I have come that they may have life and have it to the full" (Jn. 10, 10). In Christ, the Christian has an abundance that he cannot keep for himself. Of course,

53

God's grace goes beyond the visible means of mediation, the structures and preaching of the church. But what a gift for men, to know consciously the God of our Lord Jesus Christ, the mystery of his Trinitarian life, and the greatness of a love which extends from the creation to the parousia, through all the mysteries of salvation. What greater wealth than to belong to that living communion of mystics and saints who from age to age are the glory of the living church, and the guarantee of its fidelity before God? The prodigal son's older brother stayed at home and had no idea what he owed to his father and his brethren; he found it all quite natural, while his younger brother would one day experience this reality more deeply than he. There cannot be safe and secure Christians, "older brothers," who are insensitive to the spiritual anguish of the world.

EVANGELIZATION AND HUMANIZATION

Preparatory measures are necessary in nearly every field, but it can happen that these preludes or "introductions to the matter" absorb all of one's attention. The same is true of evangelization. Today we often hear of pre-evangelization, and we readily agree to both the word and the thing, provided that the prefix does not overshadow the substantive. Pre-evangelization is justified if it results in evangelization. It is praiseworthy to honor John the Baptist; but today, as before, the precursor must give place to him for whom he did but "prepare the way."

In the name of preparation and under the pretext of taking care to make a good foundation, we run the risk of becoming absorbed in the cultural, the social, the purely human. The world is judged to be as yet unready to receive the message, and we wait, doing work which we say prepares the approach. And all this while, the light is too prudently being kept under a bushel, imprisoned in silence. At Pentecost, the world of that time was certainly not ready to receive the message; nevertheless, the apostles spoke.

The world of today is perhaps not ready to listen to us. But are we really ready to speak to it? Technical and social assistance is necessary, as is cooperation toward cultural and economic development, but this necessity can never cause us to lose sight of the need and urgency to preach the gospel by the living word of God. M. D. Chenu, commenting on the phrase used by the council, "the signs of our times," has said, "Evangelization and civilization are in different orders. To feed men is, in itself, not to save them, even when my salvation demands my feeding them. To foster culture is a far different thing than converting to the faith."

We must not chase the mirage of social messianism. The Christian message, and thus the apostolate of the church, pertains first of all to the spiritual domain: Christ has said, "My kingdom is not of this world." We must distinguish between the attitude of a church anxious to contribute its total collaboration to the solution of social problems, and the attitudes of that false messianism which makes material, or at least temporal well being, the sole object of progress.

The preaching of the gospel message to the poor cannot wait upon the improvement of their social condition. On the other hand, we must recognize that that love which is the fulfillment of the law, and which is open to what is spiritual, cannot limit itself solely to what is spirit. The Christ who once refused to turn stones into bread, declaring that man does not live by bread alone, is also the Christ who fed the multitudes in the desert. It seems to me that these

55

two aspects of his life embody the twofold mission of the church.

We have to give man bread *and* the sacred host.

We have to teach the alphabet *and* the doctrine of Christ.

We must offer them social security *and* the providence of God.

We have to learn the value of work *and* the value of prayer.

We have to save not only souls, but *men*.

In brief, we must awaken within the church a sense of man and a sense of God. In order to answer fully the obligations of its mission in the world, the church must raise up social pioneers and saints.

The Urgency to be Present to the World

There is yet another sign of our times: the summons addressed to the church to be open and render itself present to the world. This serves to put the church on guard against the temptation to turn inward, toward itself, and enclose itself in a ghetto. This warning and this summons gave birth to the *Constitution on the Church in the Modern World,* which urges Christians to enter into dialogue with the world and exercise an activity which affects their times.

The conciliar concept of renewal exceeds the limits of internal reform, indispensable as this reform may be. The church serves God when it is serving man: it is at the service of the eternal God through the service of the men of the present. The aggiornamento could deviate tragically if the church, rather than open itself out to all men of today, were to content itself with addressing its own internal problems. We must be aware of the problems of today's world, and sensitive to the problems of tomorrow. Today's problems? Those of underdevelopment, hunger and war. The problems tomorrow? The coming of the post-industrial era, of a civilization of unparalleled leisure, of a technological empire which could, unless we are on guard, enslave man instead of liberating him.

The motto of Terence, "I believe that nothing human is a stranger to me," is the motto of humanism, and it applies to the church of God. The call beyond, the intimations of the future: these can protect us, or heal us, from our narrowness of vision. The church exists for today's world, and for the world of tomorrow which will undoubtedly be quite different.

Christian eschatology does not restrict itself to announcing that final day described at the end of the Apocalypse; it also invites us to prepare for it now. It urges us to go on, carrying an authentic hope, toward the generations yet to come. Eschatology, far from being an anxious fear of some future definitive calamity, is a dynamic openness to a world in the making; a world which is groaning in the throes of childbirth, waiting for the revelation of the sons of God. It is with this vision that Vatican II wished to conclude.

A COUNCIL FOR THE WORLD

In a world which is becoming more and more unified and organized on a global scale, there is no such thing as a private happening which concerns one particular group of men to the exclusion of the others. We can now apply to the great human family that which St. Paul said about the

Church of Christ: "If one member suffers all the members share the sufferings, and if one member is honored, all the members share its joy" (1 Cor. 12, 26).

The ecumenical council was primarily an intra-ecclesial event, but it quickly drew the attention of the whole human family, overreaching the distinctions of nation, culture, philosophical outlook and religious persuasion.

Undoubtedly, modern techniques of information such as radio, television and the press have contributed largely to giving this intra-ecclesial event world wide publicity. They enabled millions of men scattered over five continents to be present every day at all that went on within St. Peter's Basilica. But the fact of publicity alone does not account for the ever growing interest which the world showed in the council.

It seemed rather that as the council progressed, a dialogue developed between the church and the world beyond the collective examination of conscience which was taking place there in Rome. It was as if all of humanity were questioning itself in order better to understand the human condition and to interpret "the signs of the times." As the church's aggiornamento, which was the particular goal of the council, began to take shape and actual existence, its relevance for the whole human race became clearer.

THE MEANING OF DIALOGUE:
TO LISTEN IN ORDER TO SERVE BETTER

The human meaningfulness of the council could be summed up in these words: to listen, and to serve; more exactly, to listen in order to serve better.

In stating at the beginning of the *Constitution on the*

Church in the Modern World that "The joys and the hopes, the griefs and the anxieties of the men of this age, especially those who are poor or in any way afflicted, these too are the joys and hopes, the griefs and anxieties of the followers of Christ" (art. 4), Vatican II introduced no innovation. It did nothing but translate in more modern language the ancient commandment of Christ: "You shall love your neighbor as yourself."

Therefore, it is not the simple wish to serve humanity which constitutes the new contribution of Vatican II, but rather, the manner in which this service is understood. Vatican II goes beyond the preceding councils and shows itself to be in living union with the spirit of our time when it proclaims that to serve man means first of all to meet him and to listen to him. The council appeared within the history of the church, and of the world, as the council of dialogue.

It would be useful to consider more closely here the nature of dialogue in order to bring out its riches and promises. A dialogue has two aspects, two faces on its coin. It demands on the one hand that a person listen in order to serve better, and on the other hand that he receive in order the better to give. We will reflect a bit on these two aspects of dialogue.

To listen to the world is to open oneself to the "questions about the current trend of the world" (*Modern World*, art. 3); or as the conciliar text says elsewhere, to scrutinize "the signs of the times" (art 4). No one can deny that "Today the human race is passing through a new stage of its history. Profound and rapid changes are spreading by degrees around the whole world" (*ibid.*).

We are all involved in these changes but the important

59

thing is that we understand them. We must take hold of them so that they do not carry us along by the force of their own momentum.

To listen, then, means also to understand, to judge, to distinguish permanent values from what is merely fleeting and of the moment, to separate the truth which brings freedom from all that can lead us into a new kind of slavery. Briefly, to listen to our age is to know it clearly and sympathetically.

Then again, we must listen carefully to what the world presents for our hearing. It is a collection of things and events that is given to us as the support of our life and the context of our action. It is also the object of our activity, the work of our hands, always to be refashioned in keeping with the changes in the human condition. The world is at once a situation conferred upon us and a task which we freely assume.

THE WORLD AS SITUATION

Let us first discuss the world as situation. This is nothing else than that vast ensemble of "profound and rapid changes" which result in the fact that today the human race is passing through a new stage of its history. Among these changes there are three which are principal.

There is, first of all, the prodigious advance of science and technology. This is the fundamental factor out of which flows all the rest. This advance, since it confers upon man an ever greater control of nature, has opened up a vision of inestimable possibilities and hopes for man's liberation.

There then follows as a direct consequence of this move

forward in science and technology the unification of our planet, that is, the progressive abolition of those distances and mutual partitions which at one time separated individuals, people and cultures. There is the elimination of geographic distances due to the improved techniques of communication and information. There is the breaking down of economic and political barriers under the pressure of the need to internationalize the development and political life of nations. And finally, there is the reduction of ethnological and cultural distances because of the progress in education, the fight against illiteracy, and the greater knowledge of the various languages and customs of different people because of the daily meeting of various cultures in an atmosphere of respect and mutual aid.

But the evolution of modern techniques has also had another result. In effecting the unification of our planet it has made possible a heightened awareness of the people in the third world. This is the third great change in our modern world. It is the decisive event of our times, which Pope Paul VI has clearly delineated in the encyclical *Populorum Progressio,* which is, as it were, the *Rerum Novarum* of the 20th century.

The emergence of the third world is decisive because it signifies the awakening of the collective consciousness of the poor who still represent the very great majority of the human race. In this sense, it is the continuation on a global scale of that proletarian revolution which marked the history of the West during the latter half of the last century. The rise of the working masses in the industrialized countries and the rising of peoples in the developing nations are basically but two movements within the same historical process. It marks the appearance of the masses on the stage of the world; it is their entrance into history.

61

These three great changes: the growing power of technology, the unification of the planet, and the rise of the third world, make up one reality. They are bound to one another according to an inexorable logic and determine the direction of history. They characterize "the place and role of man in the world of today," the situation of humanity in our times.

THE WORLD AS TASK

But, as we have said, the world is also the work of man. Each new situation brings to birth new tasks. The logic within history is not of such a nature that it excludes human liberty and responsibility. This is precisely the paradox of human historical existence. It at once is within history and contributes to the making of history.

This means that the "profound and rapid changes" of which we have just spoken possess an ambivalent nature. They can turn to our good or to our ruin, depending upon our attitude toward them. Thus the liberating power of technology resides ultimately in the hands of man: everything depends upon the use he makes of it. The fact that man can use nuclear energy means that he can effect either the destruction of the human race or its progress. In the aftermath of Hiroshima, Denis de Rougemont most aptly wrote, "The bomb is not dangerous. It is but a thing . . . What is so horribly dangerous is man."

An all-powerful technocracy runs the risk of dehumanizing human society, of taking all that is sacred out of human life, of stifling what Gabriel Marcel has called "the capacity to wonder."

The same thing is true of the unification of our planet.

The multiplication of contacts between peoples and cultures can mean the enriching of human life, but it also can mean its impoverishment. Humanity could destroy itself just as effectively as by the bomb, if under the pretext of unity such a movement were to suppress creative liberty and endanger the genius proper to each culture.

The awakening of the third world is the pivotal point upon which the future will turn. It is the great hope of our times because it contains the seed of the will for greater justice and a more real equality among men. But if this hope were ever to find itself with no future, its failure could bring about the very worst of disasters. Is it not significant that Père Lebret could devote a book to the subject of the awakening of the third world under the title *The Suicide or Survival of the West*? This means that the entrance into history of countries on their way to development concerns us all.

To listen to the world is, finally, to allow oneself to be affected by the anguished cry of the great throng of the poor, of all those who hunger and thirst for a more real justice. It is to put an end to our disputes, which are as ruinous as they are scandalous, and to begin to work resolutely for the building up of a more human world, a world founded, according to the famous phrase of John XXIII in *Pacem in Terris,* upon "truth, justice, love and liberty."

The building of a more human world raises numerous and difficult problems of an economic, social and political order. It is also—and let us not forget it—a spiritual and moral task. At its depths, it means the forming of a new humanity, a humanity less egoistical, more concerned for the good of all, more conscious of its solidarity within history and of its collective responsibility. In this regard,

63

the *Constitution on the Church in the Modern World* quite appositely says, "Thus we are witnesses of a new humanism, one in which man is defined first of all by his responsibility toward his brothers and toward history" (art. 55).

"To be a man," writes Antoine de Saint-Exupéry, "is, precisely, to be responsible. It is to feel shame at the sight of what seems to be unmerited misery. It is to take pride in a victory won by one's comrades. It is to feel, when settling one's stone, that one is contributing to the building of the world."[15]

To define man in terms of his responsibility before the bar of history is to define the man of our times, the man whom we must educate both within ourselves and around us, so that he may prove himself worthy to live within the great human family on a global scale. The development of this humanism of responsibility: this, ultimately, is the great task of our century. It is a task both spiritual and moral from which no one has the right to exempt himself, the church least of all.

And this brings us to the other movement of dialogue. We have said that dialogue is an act of listening in order to serve better, an act of receiving in order the better to give, and so arises the question: what can the church bring to the world of today?

THAT WHICH THE CHURCH BRINGS TO THE WORLD

The formula could be reversed and we could ask: what is it that the world awaits from the church? One thing is

15. *Wind, Sand, and Stars,* trans. by Lewis Galantiere, New York, 1940, p. 60.

certain and it is apparent in the growing interest of the world in the work and conclusions of the council: men of today, searching for a human world, are awaiting something from the church.

But what? Certainly not that the church take upon itself the task of directing the world and claim its part within the temporal organization of the human community. In this the expectations of the world and the desires of the church correspond perfectly.

One of the great themes of the pastoral constitution on the church is precisely that the relationship of the church to the world should be thought of in terms of the legitimate autonomy of the temporal sphere. As Paul VI pointed out in an address to the Diplomatic Corps:

> The Church stands forth as entirely disengaged from any temporal interest . . . Is this to say that the Church has abandoned the world to its own destiny, for better or worse, and has retired to the desert? Quite the contrary. She separates herself from worldly pursuits only to penetrate human society more effectively, to serve the common good, to offer her help and the means of salvation to all men. She does this in such a way today as to contrast with the attitude which has characterized certain pages of her history. This is indeed a characteristic of the council, quite often revealed in it.[16]

What the men of today are awaiting from the church, and what the church desires to give them, is, in the famous phrase of Bergson, that the church be within the whole of this world as a sort of "soul supplement." For indeed, every "enlarged body," writes Bergson, awaits a "soul supplement."[17] And who can doubt that the church is able to

16. Allocution of Paul VI to the Diplomatic Corps, January 6, 1966.
17. *Les deux sources de la morale et de la religion,* Paris, 1932, p. 335.

assume this role of "soul supplement"? The church, as a living community of the disciples of Christ, is not a reality estranged from this world. As a people witnessing to Christ, itself forming part of the human family, it lives among men in a community of exchanging dialogue, in order to maintain upon this earth the living and active word of Christ.

But has not this word of Christ appeared from the very moment of its eruption in Judea and throughout all the centuries as a gospel? It is the proclamation of the good news which does not only announce good things but also makes them present and available to the degree that the message is accepted in the "obedience of faith," that is, in listening and in fidelity.

These good things are called by St. Paul the fruits of the Spirit, and he names them: "love, joy, peace, patience, kindness, goodness, fidelity, gentleness and self-control" (Gal. 5, 22–23).

As we have just heard, that which the word of Christ effects in the world through the mediation of all those who open themselves up to this word, and to the degree that they so open, is not a "flight into the desert," but rather a deep sense of who man is, a concern for men without regard to person, and a deep transformation of human relationships. It is, in effect, that very thing for which our world, searching for truth, justice and liberty, has such great need at this moment.

There is, within Christianity, a deep reverence for man, inseparable from its faith in a God who is infinitely good, and the Father of all men. For the Christian, the affirmation of God takes nothing from the greatness of man; and faith in God, when well understood, never means alienation from one's brother.

In the Christian perspective of things, respect for man, or in modern terms the recognition of man by man, has its origin ultimately in the recognition of man by God. "What is man," cries the psalmist, addressing his God in prayer, "that you remember him!"

You have made him lack but a little of God;
with glory and honour you crowned him,
gave him power over the works of your hand,
put all things under his feet" (Ps. 8, 1. 6–7).

In thus conferring upon each human person a dignity which transcends all the goods of this earth, and upon human life an infinite value, Christianity has appeared in the world as an inestimably fruitful force for humanization. It has contributed greatly to introducing and maintaining alive in the world a sacred respect for life and death, a sense of the radical equality of all human beings, and a love for truth and truthfulness ("Plain Yes or No is all you need to say," the gospel tells us). It guards an extremely elevated notion of liberty and responsibility, delicacy and gentleness in human relations, the sense of measure and repugnance for fanaticism, fidelity in love and the sacred character of the family, and the priority of work over money. In short, it contributes to that admirable harmony of spiritual and moral values whose proper role is to save the human person from the tyranny of the anonymous forces which threaten it: an excessive mechanization of human work, a totalitarian technocracy, political dictatorship, and the anonymity of a public opinion which provides the basis for demagogy.

But there is also a Christian universalism, or if you will,

a catholic dimension of Christianity. And this can aid us in resolving the difficult problem arising from the meeting of cultures in a unified world. The proper characteristic of the Christian understanding of man lies precisely in its blending together of the greatest universal comprehension with respect for the individual. Then, too, Christianity is bound to no particular culture though it is able to render all more fruitful. Christian universalism is an enriching thing. This was one of the great experiences of Vatican II, where nearly three thousand bishops coming from the most remote corners of the world worked together to update their church.

And let us say, finally, that for Christianity this sense of man is not an abstract ideology or lovely sentiment of universal sympathy lacking all contact with history. Rather, it must be the very soul and driving force of all our actions. It is the existential truth of Christianity: "If a man does not love the brother whom he has seen, it cannot be that he loves God whom he has not seen" (1 Jn. 4, 20). Or again: "But if a man has enough to live on, and yet when he sees his brother in need shuts up his heart against him, how can it be said that the divine love dwells in him? My children, love must not be a matter of words or talk; it must be genuine, and show itself in action" (1 Jn. 3, 17. 18).

And this recalls that phrase of Bernanos which so beautifully expresses the bond between love of God and the service of one's brethren: "What others are expecting of us, that is what God expects."

To love one's neighbor as oneself is thus to work for his advantage. It is, within a world which is becoming one, to assume that collective responsibility of which we have spoken and to collaborate in transforming this earth into a

68

dwelling place worthy of man, thus making of it a home for the great human family to live in truth, justice and peace. The creation of a social, political and economic regime which is more human and which answers to those desires for peace, justice, liberty and brotherhood which characterize our time: this is the task of the economists, jurists, social workers, men of state and international groups. And to join with all the spiritual and moral forces of our time in order to plant deeply within the hearts of men a respect for man: this is the task which the church desires to perform ever more perfectly and profoundly.

If, then, in the words of Paul VI, "The church detaches itself from the interests of this world," in keeping with the spirit of the council, it is solely in order the better to serve and to fulfill its role of *Mater et Magistra,* that is, of mother and teacher.

This, it seems to me, now that Vatican II is over, is the abiding dialogue between the church and the world for the future. The church believes itself to be the inheritor of spiritual riches which can make of this world a better place to live. It knows full well that it carries these treasures in earthen vessels, but the mission which has been confided to it far surpasses in grandeur the poverty of its messengers. It approaches the world of today as Peter once came to the man seated at the gate of the Temple. This man awaited from Peter some sign of fraternal concern. Peter simply said, "Silver or gold I have none; but what I have, I give you: in the name of Jesus Christ of Nazareth, arise and walk" (Acts 3, 6).

Without temporal power, lacking technical solutions, which are not its proper sphere, the church of Vatican II has but one ambition: to aid the world in freeing man from the bondage of ignorance, mistrust and fratricidal hatred, and to aid in the building, along with all men of good will, the humanism of tomorrow combining all the power of the forces of peace.

PART TWO

Coresponsibility

III.

The Coresponsibility of the Papacy

The Episcopal College and its Head

The very fact that a council was called, and the manner in which it progressed, were themselves striking expressions of coresponsibility at the highest level of the church. It was a pluralism within the realm of hierarchical responsibility. Nothing equals the eloquence of a fact. After Vatican II, no one can deny that episcopal collegiality is a living reality within the church.

It is well known, as we have pointed out above, that after Vatican I there was a backlash of opinion. Some accused the council, which had proclaimed the primacy of the pope, of having suppressed the episcopacy and of having reduced the church to an absolute monarchy dependent upon the will of one man alone.

In Germany, these reactions were particularly strong, and in 1875 the German episcopacy published an important clarification which was explicitly approved as an authentic interpretation by a brief of Pius IX. This document, which is too little known, is particularly valuable because of its balance.[1]

It is most important to understand to what degree primacy and collegiality are bound together, and to situate them in a mutual context. In his article "Primauté et collégialité au premier Concile du Vatican," Father Dejaive expresses the correlation this way:

> The successor of Peter, a bishop among bishops, because he is bound to the see of Rome, and by the fact of this heritage, is called to continue Peter's function in the church. This function is one of unifying and coordinating the pastoral activity of his brother bishops in the same faith and in the same communion, and thus to watch over the whole of the flock. His specific task as supreme pastor is, then, that of universal ruler, and this is exercised both over and within collegiality.
>
> These two propositions, over and within, express the delicate balance which characterizes the function of the sovereign pontiff. As a unifying factor, the pope is superior to the other members of the apostolic college, who only participate globally, that is, specifically and insofar as they are members of a universal pastoral care, while the pope participates as possessing a particular and personal right. His pre-eminence extends over each of the members, and over their collectivity. And this is what Vatican I wished to safeguard against the doctrinal deviations of classical Gallicanism.
>
> Nevertheless, this power, as elevated as it may be, is only exercised within a collegiality, and retains an intimate relationship with it. The pope cannot go beyond the bishops who are given to him as necessary helpers in the same way as the twelve were associated with Peter.
>
> It is certain that these two characteristics of pontifical power were always closely related. The tradition of the first centuries of

1. Cf. Dejaive, *L'Episcopat et l'église universelle,* Paris, 1962. The article by O. Rousseau (pp. 719–725) cites the relevant texts.

the church gives witness to this. The aspect of primacy was frequently underlined by the Roman see, as is the wont of authority to affirm its rights when they are sometimes misunderstood. But it is nonetheless true that papal authority was never asserted by the popes and accepted by the bishops, except in the context of solidarity, where the first of the bishops appeared as the natural leader of his brothers since he was the heir of the prerogatives of Peter. On this point, the traditions of East and West did not differ in the church as united before the schism of the 11th century.

Consequently, the pope and the bishops exercise an immediate power over the whole church. But this power is unequal, since the pope possesses it under a special title as the supreme pastor, and a bishop possesses it as a member of the episcopal body, which is only constituted a college in virtue of its principle of unity.

The relationship between the pope and the bishop is reciprocal. The bishops have power over all the church only as being within the apostolic college through their union with Peter, while the pope does not exercise his primacy except in union with the bishops, taking account of their divinely willed and preordained collaboration.

We use the expression "in union with the bishops" not in the sense of any juridical dependence upon their assent, as if their collaboration in any way limited the power of the pope. There is in this divine disposition which regulates their mutual relations absolutely no conflict of rights to be feared. And in the same way, the real power exercised by the bishops as successors of the apostles, in virtue of a divinely conferred right, in no way restricts or inhibits the plenitude of apostolic power conferred personally on Peter and his successors. The sovereign jurisdiction of the pope does not replace, but rather confirms, the apostolic power of the bishops who, remaining subordinate to him, are always necessarily associated with him.

This apostolic power of the bishops is, as we have said, an ordinary and immediate power exercised in the name of Christ: it is not a simple delegation of the personal power of the sovereign pontiff. And this last affirmation refers not only to the ordinary

75

jurisdiction of each bishop over each diocese, but also to the collegial power of the bishops over the whole church.[2]

The communion of pope and bishops is plainly visible as a result of the sessions of Vatican II. The council stressed and rendered more precise the relationship between the pope and bishops in a major text which describes episcopal collegiality:

Just as, by the Lord's will, St. Peter and the other apostles constituted one apostolic college, so in a similar way the Roman pontiff, as the successor of Peter, and the bishops, as the successors of the apostles, are joined together. The collegial nature and meaning of the episcopal order found expression in the very ancient practice by which bishops appointed the world over were linked with one another and with the bishop of Rome by the bonds of unity, charity and peace; also, in the conciliar assemblies which made common judgments about more profound matters in decisions reflecting the views of many. The ecumenical councils held through the centuries clearly attest this collegial aspect. And it is suggested also in the practice, introduced in ancient times, of summoning several bishops to take part in the elevation of someone newly elected to the ministry of the high priesthood. Hence, one is constituted a member of the episcopal body by virtue of sacramental consecration and by hierarchical communion with the head and members of the body. . . .

The order of bishops is the successor to the college of apostles in teaching authority and pastoral rule; or, rather, in the episcopal order the apostolic body continues without a break. Together with its head, the Roman pontiff, and never without this head, the episcopal order, is the subject of supreme and full power exercised over the universal Church. . . .

It is definite, however, that the power of binding and loosing,

2. *Ibid.,* pp. 655–657. For a study of many of these questions in English, cf. K. Rahner/J. Ratzinger, *The Episcopacy and the Primacy,* New York, 1962, and K. Rahner, *Bishops: Their Status and Function,* Baltimore, 1963.

which was given to Peter, was granted also to the college of apostles, joined with their head (*Constitution on the Church,* art. 22).

An ecumenical council may be a very striking expression of collegiality, but it is not its only, nor even usual, expression. Collegiality is exercised also in a normal, ongoing and daily manner by the ordinary magisterium of the church; the magisterium of the bishops scattered throughout the world. The same constitution expresses it this way:

> Although the individual bishops do not enjoy the prerogative of infallibility, they can nevertheless proclaim Christ's doctrine infallibly. This is so, even when they are dispersed around the world, provided that while maintaining the bond of unity among themselves and with Peter's successors, and while teaching authentically on a matter of faith or morals, they concur in a single viewpoint as the one which must be held conclusively (art. 25).

Doctrinal coresponsibility is expressed in that pastoral coresponsibility which is concerned with the good of a whole church. The Second Vatican Council reminded bishops that if their pastoral jurisdiction is exercised over only that portion of the people of God which is confided to them, they nevertheless are all members of the episcopal college and successors of the apostles. Under this twofold title, they must carry in their hearts a care for the universal church. All of the bishops must further the unity and progress of the faith, the discipline common to the whole church, the preaching of the gospel throughout the whole world, and the expansion of missionary activity. Those priests whom the bishops release from their own dioceses in order to allow them to take part in the evangelization of the whole world, and who for this reason are called "*fidei donum,*" are

77

one of the visible and practical expressions of this universal coresponsibility.

Pope Paul VI in an allocution of December 6, 1965, addressed to the Italian bishops, just before the end of the council, said:

It seems to us that episcopal authority stands firmly established in its divine institution and confirmed by the council. The council restated the value of the pastoral power of bishops in regard to teaching, sanctifying and governing; and we see this episcopal authority adorned by its extension to the universal church, in virtue of collegial communion. This same episcopate had its place more clearly defined within the hierarchy, and was strengthened by fraternal coresponsibility with other bishops in regard to the universal and particular needs of the church, and was more closely associated in a spirit of a well-ordered union and close collaboration with the head of the church, the constitutive center of the episcopal college.

And a little later, on the occasion of consecrating four new bishops, on March 19, 1966, the pope expressed the dimensions of episcopal collegiality this way:

And you, newly consecrated bishops, after having felt the weight of the gospel book upon your shoulders, did you not hear these solemn words: "Receive the gospel, and go preach to the people . . ." And you know how the ecumenical council, when it proclaimed the powers of the bishops, recalled at the same time their duties: the episcopacy is a responsibility, even more a coresponsibility as wide as the world.

Too easily, an opposition is established between the pope acting alone, and the pope acting as head, within episcopal collegiality. All of these declarations show clearly that if the primacy is in fact a prerogative of the sovereign pontiff, there

78

can be no question of his governing the church without the collaboration of the episcopacy. And this means that the greater and more active role played by the episcopacy, the more each particular church will be able to develop its own spiritual personality, the more the Christian people will mature in a greater diversity of rites, theologies, disciplines and customs, and the papal primacy will be free to exercise fully its specific role of assuring the fundamental unity and cohesion of the church.

The *Constitution on the Church* tells us that "the Roman pontiff, as the successor of St. Peter, is the perpetual and visible source and foundation of the unity of the bishops and the multitude of the faithful" (art. 23). This is the *raison d'être* of the primacy. During the next few generations, as all the regions of the world grow in their variety and diversity, according to the desire expressed by the conciliar decrees themselves, the true role of the papal primacy will appear to us as something both providential and necessary. This very primacy will be revealed as the protector of diversity and guarantor of unity.

Coresponsibility and the Synod of Bishops

Coresponsibility, then, pertains to the very structure of the church, but its actual practice in regard to the hierarchy can assume many forms according to historical circumstances. We are not treating here of the divinely conferred aspects of the episcopacy or those things which pertain to the very essence of the church, but rather of their concrete applications. And this is subject to development and revision.

The council gave existence to a new organism pertaining to this realm of contingent concretization: the world synod of bishops. Before the convocation of the council, the central preparatory commission had already expressed the idea of establishing within the church a sort of "limited permanent council." At the council itself several of the fathers asked for an institution within the ordinary governing body of the church which would facilitate collaboration between the bishops and the pope, under his authority.

As we know, Pope Paul VI took the initiative in establishing the world synod of bishops. He announced his intention at the beginning of the fourth session of Vatican II. As defined by the motu proprio of September 15, 1965, the synod is conceived as a permanent institution in the church. That is to say, it is permanent as an institution: its members are chosen principally by the episcopal conferences for a limited time, according to various needs, and with a view to specific problems.

The synod, as we have it, is conceived as a purely consultative body, and in this it differs from the concept held by its promoters at the council. It responds to the matters put before it, and only to those. There is no question of a "miniature council"—an ambiguous expression at best—because at a council all the bishops of the world are convoked, and they are there with the full right of deliberative vote. These differences are essential.

Some theologians saw in the synod a collegial reality which, even though not conciliar, could exercise power over the universal church. Others contested this view, saying that there is question here only of an assistance asked by the pope in the exercise of his primacy of power. It seems to me that this second opinion is the true one, but that a

THE CORESPONSIBILITY OF THE PAPACY

development is not only possible but desirable. At the present moment the synod is a place where the pope can "go and think," and it does not have any deliberative power. This synod has nothing in common with those synods known to the Eastern church. It is not specifically an expression of collegiality even though "existentially" it is such an expression by the very fact that it arises out of Vatican II, the council of collegiality. It seems best, then, to restrict ourselves to the definition given by Cardinal Marella: "The synod could be defined as a symbol or sign of collegiality, but it is certainly not an expression of actual collegiality in a doctrinal sense as is, for example, an ecumenical council."

These juridical distinctions have their importance, but the decisive value of the world synod of bishops lies in the possibility that it opens for a fuller collaboration between the pope and the bishops present at the synod representing the episcopacy of the world. Life itself is always richer and more fruitful than law.

The first world synod of bishops took place in Rome from the 29th of September through the 29th of October 1967. In opening the synod the pope said that he awaited from the bishops there present "the help, support and counsel which we hope to receive in greater measure from the bishops in our apostolic ministry."

A backward glance at the synod will allow us to draw up a balance sheet, indicating both its assets and its deficiencies. First and foremost, the existence of the synod, something unthinkable before the council, marks a significant point in the development of the church. To use the expression of Cardinal Conway, co-president of the synod, "We have made a test flight, the plane has taken off and landed again without difficulty. Now we must improve its performance." This will mean tuning the motor more delicately, improving the capacity for acceleration, and more clearly defining the route of the flight.

The composition of the synod and the interventions made there constantly highlighted the importance of the role of the episcopal conferences. The bishops who were at the synod were not, as at a council, there as individual persons, but as delegates, elected by their peers in a secret vote. They were there incarnating that special type of full responsibility implied in every episcopal conference. This is a very significant fact. The members of the synod were not forbidden to speak in their own name, but they were asked to indicate this explicitly when they made personal interventions. Such interventions were the exception, and each bishop was presumed to be the representative of the bishops of his country and region.

It was agreed that general laws are most valuable for the whole church whether it be a question of canon law, priestly education, liturgy or catechetical directorate. But it was also stressed that these laws should be more of the nature of general principles, sufficiently broad and supple to admit diversity of context and particular traditions, and to allow the local or regional bishops greater latitude in applying them. This is a good example of the principle of subsidiarity, so often invoked at the council, according to which each authority should assume full responsibility at its own level for those things which pertain to its competence.

The synod strongly accentuated the pluralism of the church. For nearly every question highlighted two contributions, that of the head and that of the rest of the body there present, and these were brought to a meeting in order to find harmony. It seemed that regional or even continental pluralism was a very solid reality determining certain options common to the nations as a whole. This reality will most probably be called upon to play a greater role in the further development of the synod.

If the synod of 1967 shows many important assets on its balance sheet, it is also true that it was the object of some criticism, both from within and from without. From without, Christian opinion reproached the synod for not having considered the burning questions of our day which affect both people and clergy: birth control, optional celibacy and the great problems of the world which weigh on men, such as the underdevelopment of two-thirds of the world. The synod seemed to be concerned only with the internal order of the church, and did not readily appear as relevant to a church open to the world. Then too, the synod was criticized by the world press which felt frustrated by the lack of communication and information.

To these reactions from without, which we recount here in the name of objectivity, one could add a certain number of observations made from those who lived the synod. These latter were asked to make their ideas known in order to aid in the direction and development of the institution.

It seems to us that the success of similar meetings in Rome will depend to a large degree upon the work which prepares for them. A preliminary consultation made in writing on the themes which are to be studied, with a classification of the responses, and a synthesis elaborated by experts, would permit a more fruitful exchange of ideas and more profitable debates.

There was too long a succession of monologues, an

83

absence of theologians representing diverse tendencies in the church, and the matter to be considered was divided into workshops; all of this must be reviewed and better organized. If collaboration is to be effective, then all must be able to profit by the experience of the collaborators. Without doubt, this will be the task of a permanent secretariat working during the interval between synods to gather and organize the various suggestions. It will also be necessary to avoid too rigid a structure. Even at the council, the structure was modified after the experience of the first session. Such adaptation should be easier at the synod since it is not as large a body as the council.

It is perfectly normal that an institution as new as this one should require some time to adjust all its moving parts and should need periodical overhauling. It will be up to sociologists and pastoral specialists to indicate how similar meetings in the world of today can be held in such a way that we avoid a feeling of frustration among the men of our time, and among our fellow Christians, while still according to those participating in the synod the right of dedicating time and study to the internal problems of the church. The mass media have to find, in common accord with authority, a means of respecting both the legitimate demands of information and the right to privacy required by certain deliberations. No one, for example, demands a complete account of what takes place at a cabinet meeting or at a meeting of heads of state. There has to be some balance found between a necessary discretion and the desire for openness characteristic of the church and the world today; something like the formula found in Vatican II beginning with the second session. Such a balance is all the more necessary now that the people of God are consciously concerned with the problems of the church. This growing awareness on their part brings with it the right not to be deceived insofar as this depends on us.

Theologians must discover the relationship between the synod and that collegiality which is of divine institution, drawing from this latter some of its implied practical applications. Canonically speaking, the synod as it is now conceived does not derive from episcopal collegiality. Nevertheless, collegiality remains an immanent factor in the structure of the church. Life itself must find the balance between these two realities: integral respect for a divinely conferred primacy within the church, and full realization of an authentically exercised collegiality.

Episcopal Coresponsibility and the College of Cardinals

In order to determine adequately the meaning and the role of the synod, we must situate it in regard to another important institution in the church, namely, the college of cardinals, which also has the role of counseling the pope. This is a delicate and complex problem, but one which interests the whole church, since, according to present legislation, it is the college of cardinals which elects the pope, and thus, indirectly at least, determines the general orientation of the church's pastoral activity in the world.

We will restrict ourselves here to presenting certain facts which can aid in clarifying the search for solutions. Everyone recognizes that pontifical authority is a manifold function, or more exactly, that it includes various functions of unequal importance accruing to it under various titles.

85

The pope is, in fact, at one and the same time the bishop of Rome, the primate of Italy, the archbishop and metropolitan of the Roman province, the patriarch of the West, and shepherd of the universal church. This diversity of functions conditions the specific roles of the various collaborators with the sovereign pontiff.

The role of the sacred college in particular has been strongly influenced by the ebb and flow of history. In the early centuries of the church, the bishop of Rome, as all the bishops, was surrounded by a college of presbyters. Thus, given the importance of the apostolic see, the clergy of Rome found itself at times involved in pastoral problems of a wider scope.[3] And when the papal throne was vacant, this presbyterium had to concern itself with current ecclesiastical affairs and maintain contact with the churches which had had recourse to the bishop of Rome. Finally, certain deacons, priests and even bishops of the region around Rome constituted a college around the pope. This college saw its importance progressively grow after 1059 when Nicholas II accorded to it the exclusive right of electing the pope of Rome. Because of the conflicts between the papacy and the German emperors during the 12th century, and as a result of the political activity of certain of its members who acted as negotiators and legates, the college of cardinals succeeded in obtaining such a great share in the general administration in the church as to place itself above the episcopacy. The practice of holding Roman synods was abandoned, and the pope became accustomed to treating more important questions with the cardinals as they met in consistory several times a week. Utilizing the

3. Under certain aspects, this calls to mind the "permanent Synods" of the East.

concept of "*corporatio*," the canonists of the 13th century arrived at the conclusion that the pope is the head of the Roman church and the cardinals are its members: together they "represent" the apostolic see.

From the 16th century onward, this form of collegial activity progressively deteriorated. The bull *Postquam Verum* of Sixtus V (December 3, 1586) installed the Roman curia and provided that various matters be referred to the different cardinal-directed congregations with the pope alone making the final decision. It was not only with Pius IX that the consistory as a counseling body lost all real meaning.

In keeping with these historical developments, there was a corresponding theological oscillation in regard to the cardinalate. At the moment when the "cardinals" were at the height of their influence, Pope Eugene IV explained that they had precedence over the bishops because "the pope is the vicar and living image of Jesus Christ, and the college of cardinals represents the sacred college of the apostles around Jesus Christ, whereas the bishops represent the same apostles scattered throughout the world for the spreading of the gospel."

There were theologians like Torquemada who maintained and tried to prove that the cardinalate was of divine institution ("The apostles were first cardinals rather than bishops"), and that the cardinalate constituted, after the pope, the highest level of ecclesiastical hierarchy. No one today would dare propose such opinions. In fact, it is surprising that they were ever maintained without being condemned.

At least these old controversies served to show that there was no unambiguous definition regarding the nature of the college of cardinals. At the moment, the relationship between this college and the synod of bishops is not perfectly clear, and its representative character in regard to the universal church is far from being established.

After the last consistory, the total number of cardinals was 120, of whom 37 were Italians. However, it is especially the pyramid of age groups within this college which has created a problem of aggiornamento in the postconciliar church. If we analyze this total of 120 cardinals, we obtain the following results:

24 cardinals are between 81 and 95 years of age,
44 cardinals are between 71 and 80 years of age,
35 cardinals are between 61 and 70 years of age,
17 cardinals are less than 60 years old.

The problem of age limit foreseen in the recent reform of the curia presents itself as well in regard to all the cardinals. Assuredly, the experience conferred by age has its value. But if the church is fully to realize its mission in the world, while experiencing at the same time an ongoing process of development, and if it is to be able to resolve the new and grave pastoral problems presented by this situation, there must be on the part of its leaders an openness and availability for dialogue which the weight of years renders more difficult despite great good will and talent.

This problem deserves attentive study and its resolution is important. Given the determining role of the sacred college in the election of a pope, it is desirable that a matter so fraught with consequence for the whole people of God be studied by the world synod of bishops, and by consultation with the various episcopal conferences.

Coresponsibility of Bishops
and the Roman Curia

The council did not only desire the institution of a world council—which received the name of episcopal synod; it also expressed the desire to see various departments of the Roman curia reformed in the same perspective of complete openness.

The conciliar *Decree on the Bishops' Pastoral Office of the Church* gave expression to this desire in these words:

> The fathers of this most sacred council strongly desire that these departments—which have rendered exceptional assistance to the Roman pontiff and to the pastors of the church—be reorganized and better adapted to the needs of the times, and of various regions and rites. This task should give special thought to their number, name, competence and particular method of procedure, as well as to the coordination of their activities. The fathers also eagerly desire that, in view of the pastoral role proper to bishops, the office of legates of the Roman pontiff be more precisely determined.
>
> Furthermore, since these departments are established for the good of the universal Church, this council wishes that their members, officials and consultors, as well as legates of the Roman pontiff, be drawn more widely from various geographical areas of the church, insofar as it is possible. In such a way the offices and central agencies of the Catholic church will exhibit a truly universal character. It is also desired that into the membership of these departments there be brought other bishops, especially diocesan ones, who can more adequately apprise the supreme pontiff of the thinking, the desires and the needs of all the church (arts. 9 and 10).

Pope Paul responded to the appeal of the council by promulgating a constitution on the reform of the Curia entitled *Regimine Ecclesiae Universae,* on August 15, 1967.

The pope has the intention, as did Pius X in 1908, to put an end to the confusion of competencies, the overlapping of legislative, executive and judiciary functions, which too often have impeded the exercise of the curial structure so as to make of it a more supple and serviceable instrument under his authority. Thus lifetime tenure of major offices has been replaced by a tenure of five years.

The most striking innovation in regard to episcopal responsibility has been the introduction in each of the Roman congregations of seven residential bishops. It is still too early to appreciate the importance and value of this measure. All will depend upon how active a role these bishops will play within each congregation, the importance of the questions submitted for their consideration, and the regularity of their meetings. This insertion of residential bishops will undoubtedly be a very fruitful occasion for actualizing collaboration between the entire church and the center.

Up to this point, cardinals residing outside of Rome have been attached to Roman congregations. But it was a purely formal relationship; their participation in the work of the congregation was almost nil, and their title as member of the congregation remained more or less theoretical. The manner of making consultations must also be revised.

In speaking of the "seeds of life" which Vatican II planted in the soil of the church, Paul VI was undoubtedly thinking also of the growing exercise of coresponsibility at the level of the universal church, a development which is in progress and which is a source of joy. It bears within itself riches for the life of the post-conciliar church, and for the future of ecumenism, which will be conditioned largely by the practical and concrete translation in daily life of the great inspirations and movements which Vatican II has fostered.

IV.

The Coresponsibility
of Bishops

Two Perspectives

There are ways of approaching the mystery of the church, two different but complementary perspectives we can adopt when considering it. One can start from the universal church considered as a whole, and then go on to discover the place of the particular local church in relation to this whole. This is the usual perspective of the Western church, and it is at the basis of Latin ecclesiology.

One can also consider first of all the local churches, "the church of God which is at Corinth," at Ephesus or at Antioch. Beginning with this point of view, one could consider the structure of the church as a communion of particular churches, bound to a center of communion and unity—the bishop of Rome. This is the perspective of Eastern ecclesiology; it is the line of growth followed by history.

As we all realize, the initial point of view of each of these theologies is of great importance when it comes to ecumenism. That is why Western theologians today accentuate more and more that aspect of the church under which it is seen as a communion of churches taking into account all the implications of this perspective.

THE INDIVIDUAL CHURCH

It was to be expected that Vatican II would accentuate the importance of the local or particular church. The universal church is not primarily a society of individuals, nor is it a conglomeration of units joined directly to the head. It is rather a body with organs each having its own proper characteristics; it is a communion of churches which together form the "catholic" church. St. Paul sometimes speaks of the church, and sometimes of the churches. The Eastern liturgy prays for the "peace and prosperity of the holy churches of God and for the unity of all men." This perspective avoids the danger of an exclusively individualistic conception of the church.

Then too, the local churches contain, as actualized and revealed in themselves, the mystery of the unique church of Christ. They are the concrete, historical and spatial incarnation of the one mystery of this church. And this is why tradition does not speak of the churches *of* Ephesus, *of* Corinth or *of* anywhere else, but rather in the singular "of the church which is *at* Ephesus, Corinth, etc." The Christian communities, no matter where they may be, are "one" because they possess the greatest unifying factors: identity of faith, agreement in regard to morality, and a

93

common baptism, eucharist and hope. And thus constituted under the leadership of each bishop, each local community lives and manifests the essential unity of the church.

As a matter of fact, the *universal* church is the dominant perspective of the *Constitution on the Church*. This is partly explained by the realities that it considers, especially the episcopal college and the papacy, and their relationship to the universal church most especially. We are all aware of the contrary tendencies present at the council in regard to papal power and the power of the episcopal college: a synthesis was sought by considering the term of these powers. As a result, the council did not fully accord to the "particular churches" the place that they have in the Christian conception of the church. However, if the *Constitution on the Church* is too sparing in its remarks on this point, the *Decree on the Bishops' Pastoral Office in the Church* expresses itself quite clearly:

A diocese is the portion of God's people which is entrusted to a bishop to be shepherded by him with the cooperation of the presbytery. Adhering thus to its pastor and gathered together by him in the Holy Spirit through the gospel and the eucharist, this portion constitutes a particular church in which the one, holy, catholic and apostolic church of Christ is truly present and operative (art. 11).

This manner of stressing the place of particular churches is very valuable. It prevents us from imposing upon the church a notion of society which does violence to its divine reality. When we treat of the church, we must free ourselves from images and concepts too casually adopted from profane sociology. The church is a mystery illuminated by the mystery of the Trinity from which it draws its life: analogies made between the church and civil society require constant corrective thinking.

THE CHURCHES UNITED IN AN EPISCOPAL CONFERENCE

Now we are equally aware that a particular church does not exist within the church as a whole as some self-sufficient and isolated reality. The episcopal consecration is conferred by a consecrating bishop and two co-consecrating bishops, witnessing by this fact alone to the solidarity which exists between the churches. In times gone by, bishops sent to one another, as a symbol of their brotherhood, a fragment of the eucharist which they had consecrated, and a copy of their common profession of faith. "Horizontal" collegiality has become today, as never before, a requirement of pastoral activity.

Each particular church is beginning to understand more profoundly its duty to be open and to communicate with its sister churches in the same area, but we still have progress to make in this regard. The idea of coresponsibility among the bishops was clearly stated during the council, which was itself a good example of this very reality. There were, no doubt, before the council, episcopal conferences composed of bishops of the same region or country, but generally speaking these conferences did not have a real status. The council gave to these conferences a new inspiration, a wider scope and more precise tasks. It opened up the way for a great decentralization within the church.

The movement did not stop at national boundaries. We now have conferences on a continental scale. Even before the council, Latin America possessed CELAM, which was a grouping of the bishops of the whole continent, and now other similar conferences have arisen. Rome was the birth-place of the episcopal conferences of Europe and of Africa which are now in their beginning stages.

In his greeting to the first assembly of European bishops, which met in Holland during the summer of 1967, the papal secretary of state, Amleto Cardinal Cicognani, wrote in the name of the pope:

> It is with joy that his Holiness greets this actualized awareness of pastoral solidarity, so much in keeping with the episcopal col-legiality highlighted by the recent council. He is delighted to perceive here a reality which is not only useful but necessary today in the church for the integral accomplishment of its mission.

This meeting enabled all present to share in all the things being experienced during the course of the synod of priests and the diocesan pastoral council. Admittedly, these at-tempts at organization were but at their beginnings. Never-theless, the mutual exchange was appreciated by all. Another meeting of the bishops of Europe is scheduled for July 1969 in Switzerland. A tradition has begun which promises well for the future.

This widening of horizons summons each bishop to think in terms of church before thinking of the diocese, or rather, to think church in order the better to think diocese.

There was a very vivid sense of coresponsibility among the early church fathers. Ignatius of Antioch wrote to the churches of Asia in order to strengthen them in their faith around their own shepherds. Polycarp of Smyrna wrote to the church of Philippi in Macedonia. Eusebius, in his *Ecclesiastical History,* speaks of the solicitude of Denis of Corinth as something quite normal. Denis, he wrote, was "not content to exercise the zeal of God in regard to those who were under his authority, but tirelessly extended it even to other places." He tells us of the letters Denis wrote to the Lacedemonians, the Athenians, the Nicomedians and the Cretes, and to the churches of Amasty, Pontus and Cnossos.

The ministry in the church is a "power" but a power for service. Ancient tradition willingly placed accent on the idea of the service to be rendered for the common good, without denying the reality of the ministerial charism proper to each bishop in regard to the church confided to him.

This openness to others is an integral and living part of the communion of the churches. There is always the temptation to be turned in on oneself. But in our time, when problems and ideas rapidly become a worldwide concern, we must accept full responsibility for universalism. "All the sufferings of the world concern us directly," someone once said, and this is true for each church no matter where it may be. The lot of any church is a common concern. The council reminds us that the "solicitude for all the churches" of which St. Paul speaks must be shared by all. Solicitude and jurisdiction are not synonymous, nor are they co-extensive.

This rapid glance over the possibilities which lie open to episcopal coresponsibility invite all of us to question ourselves in regard to some new demands which involve the exercise of authority. We are expected to accept these new demands made upon our sense of responsibility.

AN EXAMINATION OF CONSCIENCE

During the meeting of European bishops which we mentioned before, Bishop Marty of Rheims made a very moving public examination of conscience in regard to the manner in which he had assumed his episcopal responsibility before the council, and his conduct since then. He spoke with humor and humility, contrasting his two successive attitudes, his passage from a certain unconscious paternalism and friendly condescendence, to a direct and open dialogue, as is fitting in our time.

All of us there recognized himself in this picture of times gone by. Each of us understood that the profound dogmatic reality of episcopal authority, while remaining unchanged in itself, has been obliged to assume new aspects within the contemporary context. But, let us admit it, this psychological transition does not take place overnight. There must be allowance made for a time of trial and error, and research. What is most important is the general orientation which one adopts and which governs the options made in particular circumstances.

There is no course given to prepare one as an organizer of diocesan pastoral effort. We were taught many things at the seminary, but there were no classes on the techniques of organizing a diocese, or of a parish for that matter. There were no lectures on group dynamics, on the laws of collective psychology, or on how to calculate future trends.

The criticisms leveled against diocesan structures, against their impersonalism or anonymity, are too constant and too worldwide not to merit attentive study. For if the system can be corrected, more or less, by the way men act within it, it is still true that the system itself suffers from internal deficiencies which must be remedied. This demand is all the more urgent since pastoral activity, which until yesterday was exercised in an extremely individualistic climate, is becoming more and more structured and coordinated.

This presupposes a systematic convergence of effort, a mutual collaboration in an atmosphere of confidence, and an animating presence of a new type.

The demands made on us are manifold:

> Modern pastoral activity requires teamwork, that is, a collaboration with others who are entrusted with real responsibility.

> This activity, which must constantly adapt itself to new situations and meet a world in the process of change, requires that all engaged in it, especially its directors, have the opportunity for study and renewal in some form or another.

> We must consult modern techniques: the laws of organization and structure, and efficiency.

> Our modern pastoral situation poses with particular insistence the problem of regular replacement of personnel.

Let us now consider these various demands in particular.

The Sharing of Responsibilities. In every field today, teamwork is the predominant characteristic. Whether it be a matter of an Apollo space program, medical research to find a cure for leukemia, or a question of military, economic or social organization, the task of the leader has become so complex that he is really more a coordinator, an orchestra leader, than a man who should know and solve all problems. Today's pastoral effort will be a team effort, or it will be neither pastoral nor successful.

Everywhere today men condemn an individualism which rejects cooperation, and this means there is less place than ever for this type of thinking in the church of the Lord. Men

99

have discovered the meaning and value of a common united effort. They have understood that "it takes many to be intelligent," and we must avail ourselves of this insight.

However, these human reasons, valuable as they may be, are not the profound reason which elicits collaboration within the church. "The church is a communion," and this fundamental dogmatic truth must characterize the direction and the practice of modern pastoral concern. The mystery of communion has assumed various forms throughout the history of the church, but today one thing is certain: the era of absolute monarchy is over, and authority must be exercised within a new sociological context.

Renewal for Those in Charge. The world's life rhythm moves with dazzling speed. For thousands of years men moved with the speed of a horse or a camel, traveling a few miles an hour. Within the last hundred years, speed of travel has grown in geometric proportions. Today men can move at speeds near 25,000 miles per hour, and tomorrow, newspapers will tell us that even these records have been surpassed.

Speed is but a symbol. What is true for the speeds at which man can move, is true in every domain. Many areas of human endeavor are renewed every five or ten years: it would be criminal for a doctor to treat his patients relying only on the knowledge he had when he graduated; and an industry which does not adapt, disappears.

The church is a supernatural mystery whose roots are in eternity. We cannot offer superficial change as sacrifice to the gods of today, idols which succeed one another like waves upon a beach. There is a presence of the eternal

100

which must be guarded intact. Yet the church addresses its message to men who live, as it does, within a world which is evolving. It must address itself to each succeeding generation, bringing the word of life to progressive sociological contexts, and responding to men's constant questions. At the core of this passing on of the gospel message there is a perpetual dialogue, a living word addressing itself to living men.

The gospel must be translated in a language that speaks. And we may not consider that this "bringing up to date" is, as the words might imply, no more than supplying for a time lag: the necessity for translation moves with the rhythm of life itself. We were taught that *vita est in motu* ("life is movement"). How can we hope to return to a status quo which is changing with every step we take? There must be, then, theological and pastoral adaptation, both informed and intense, for those in charge of pastoral activity: they must attend workshops and courses for renewal. Our modern day shows us leaders in the industrial and military worlds going back periodically to school, and one way or the other we must do the same.

Utilization of Techniques. The progress of the human sciences and the understanding of human relations has arrived at such a level that the pastoral dimension of the church's life must utilize all the positive factors in this domain in order to bring out the value of work done in common, organizing it and allowing it to yield its full potential. From now on, the insights achieved in the techniques of group dynamics or group dialogue must be part of our pastoral equipment.

To refuse any recourse to these techniques under the

101

pretext that the church's pastoral activity pertains to the supernatural, would be to sin by a false supernaturalism and to misunderstand the laws of a sane anthropology. Of course, the goal of the church's pastoral activity pertains to the realm of faith, and it is faith which passes ultimate judgment on those means which lead to the goal. Then too, since the Christian apostolate is ultimately concerned with the kingdom of God, whatever is undertaken in this domain depends radically upon the free and gratuitous grace of the Lord as its source, and has as its ultimate term a completely fulfilled life with the Lord.

However, in the actual working out of those things which we call "means"—whether they be of divine institution like the sacraments, or simply technical aids like loudspeakers—there is always present, to a greater or less degree, a human aspect which follows the laws of human nature, of psychology and sociology. A car will never move an inch when it is out of gas, but all the good will in the world on the part of the driver will move the car no further even if its tank is full unless he has the ignition key. So too, the apostolate must be nourished by a spiritual life. If it does not draw its strength from the theological virtues, it is destined, like a car without gas, never to move. But for there to be "ignition contact," the laws of human communication must also be respected.

There are many discoveries yet to be made in this field, which has hardly been explored, and which has received the name of apostolic methodology. Laymen are vividly aware of this need, and they can contribute greatly to filling it. To give but one example: it seems to us that the organization of the council would have produced greater dialogue and greater fruit if, beforehand, those techniques of discussion and the working out of projects which are a feature of any great worldwide organization, had been more thoroughly studied and adopted. It is easy to see how the field for the application of these techniques, which facilitate human life and conduct, could be expanded in many directions.

Retirement. Finally, since today's world continually offers a series of new problems, it is necessary that the leaders, burdened with responsibilities incomparably heavier than those of yesteryear, be endowed with a physical and mental vigor which has not been required to the same degree before. In an interview given just before he left for New York, Pope Paul VI underlined the contrast between our age and former ages in these words:

When I was at Milan, I saw the archives of the diocese for the time of St. Charles Borromeo. The problems which then arose were the buying of a confessional, repairing a church, the presence of three drunkards in the parish, and the activities of a sorceress. Today the situation is completely different. There is no longer question of some sorceress bothering the people, but rather of millions who no longer believe in God.

A chart which would compare the work for a bishop or a priest half a century ago and the work of a bishop or priest today would, no doubt, be most enlightening. It follows that those responsible today must face up to the problem of retirement—a problem which has never been as acute as it is today.

At the council, we considered ourself obliged to point out this serious problem of retirement. We would like to be permitted here, even at the risk of repetition, to cite the text of our intervention:

103

I wish to speak in favor of the age limit to be introduced. When the preparatory commission for *"De Episcopis,"* of which I was a member, began discussion on this delicate topic, nearly all the members declared themselves opposed to an age limit imposed by law. But when the long and profound discussion had reached its term, the *"longe maior pars"* ("by far the greater majority"), as the secretary has well reported, declared themselves in favor of a defined age limit, determined by law.

This evolution of thought within the commission itself invites us to reflect a bit. The question is delicate: no one is a good judge in his own case. It is a question which cannot be solved solely by recourse to theology. In opposition to a well-defined age limit, the concept of episcopal paternity was appealed to, and there were those who invoked the indissoluble nature of the marriage contract, as it is called, between the bishop and his people and clergy. Let us not urge these principles too strongly: this assembly counts many bishops who have been transferred many times from their episcopal sees. And also, while a father always remains a father, responsibility for the direction of undertakings within the family passes gradually to the son. Doubtless, the considerations put forward in favor of the permanence of the episcopal office have their value, but the gospel and tradition invite us to have recourse to other principles which are at least as valid, and even decisive, in favor of the opposite opinion. Is not the episcopal ministry first and foremost a service? Is it not completely subordinated to the good of souls? We are dealing here, then, with a pastoral problem.

In the light of this pastoral exigency, we would wish to insist on the necessity of introducing a clearly defined norm. To limit oneself, as does the text proposed to the council, to a pious exhortation to retire one day, would be to strike a sword blow on water. Everyone knows that the situation would be unlikely to change very greatly. We must efficaciously will what we desire, and pay the price. If the council is a council of pastoral renewal, then this renewal should begin with the bishops, cardinals included.

Vatican II will take its place in history as the council of bishops. They will receive great responsibility, and it is only logical to conclude that where responsibility grows greater, the demands implied in assuming it grow equally greater. Today, the role of the bishop has become heavier and heavier. He is not only a pontiff who governs a diocese, as in days gone by; he has become more and more the animator and indispensable coordinator of all the pastoral activity of his diocese. He is the man who must train his clergy, the religious, the apostolic movements, and the laity, in order to place the church as a whole in its missionary reality.

Such a role demands physical forces that are intact.

The sociological rhythm of the world moves it along at an accelerated pace. Totally new problems arise, and one must be constantly renewed if one wishes to keep the confidence of his people and clergy and respond to the call of the Holy Spirit in our times. After a certain age, despite the good will of the bishop, a distance, a gap, is opened which can be very harmful to the good spirit of the diocese.

Is there anyone among us who does not know those painful situations due to the over-advanced age of a bishop still in office? These are the types of situations we must visualize if we are to judge correctly.

Then too, let us not forget, our pastoral duty demands that we ask a pastor who is over-age to retire for the good of his parish. Think of what type of situation would arise for the bishop, if the priest could answer him, or think in silence, "Physician, heal yourself!"

As we know, the faithful are paying very great attention to the reaction of the council to this point. They consider it the most certain indication of a serious desire for a pastoral renewal. Let us not scandalize them. We must remember too that in the domains of the civil, scientific, university and diplomatic life, an age limit has been introduced notably lower than ours, so that the common good may be better served. The faithful will not understand why the common good of souls does not require similar measures. It is true that the episcopacy is not a reality of the natural order, but in order that this role may be fulfilled, the laws of human psychology are still relevant, and the demands of the supernatural common good are more serious than others.

Because of his unique position and the very requirements of the common good of the church, what we have just said does not apply to the supreme head of the church. Certain exceptions to the law are conceivable also in those cases where a bishop would now find himself near the age of retirement, without having made proper preparations. Finally, it is possible that the sociological conditions of the Eastern churches do not require this solution with the same urgency. But, having said this, it still seems to me that the good of souls requires that there be precise legislation in this matter with the sovereign pontiff to be the judge when an exception is to be made in a special case.

In case the council does not accept the proposition which I offer here of an age limit of 75 years, then let it at least decide that, at that age, a bishop receive the right to a coadjutor. In such a case let the bishop stay in his place and be treated with all the regard due to him, but let the coadjutor gradually take over the direction of the diocese. The Holy See could, in this hypothesis, confer upon the coadjutor greater or less powers in accord with each concrete situation. In this way, it seems to me, we can take account of the various aspects which must be synthesized here, in order to arrive at pastoral renewal, which is the very reason for this council.

It goes without saying that there is room here to provide fittingly for the livelihood of a retired bishop, and to enunciate some of its conditions within the text to be voted upon.

As we know, the council expressed its agreement with this principle, but did not determine it concretely. Since then a new step has been taken in the direction indicated. Pope Paul VI, in his motu proprio *Ecclesiae Sanctae*, decreed as follows:

To implement prescription no. 21 of the *Decree on the Pastoral Office of Bishops*, all diocesan bishops and others who are their equals by law are urgently requested voluntarily to submit their resignation to the competent authority no later than at the age of 75. After looking into the circumstances of each case, the authority will make proper provision.

A bishop whose resignation has been accepted can maintain a residence in the diocese if he so desires. The diocese must provide suitable and fitting support for a bishop who resigns. In general, it is up to the episcopal conferences of the territory to determine the basis on which dioceses should carry out this obligation.

The practical implementation of these directives will be an indication of the progress of pastoral renewal.

V.

The Coresponsibility of Priests

The Priest in Today's Church

THE PRIEST OF ALL TIMES AND THE PRIEST OF TODAY

During this period of rapid changeover and increasing dechristianization, it is to be expected that the priest, along with every Christian, should ask himself about his place in the world. But because the priest will always be a Christian in a particular way, a privileged witness of the ecclesial community, it is also to be expected that he be especially attentive to the questions which the church is asking itself today. He is associated in a very unique way with the search for answers that this implies.

The problem of the priest is inherent in his function: to be leaven in the dough is a task at once paradoxical and delicate, because it involves the bringing together of contraries. In order to be leaven the priest must be close, very close, to men. Leaven which is placed but a fraction of an inch from the dough, can have no effect. But if the leaven loses its own character, that is, if it loses its capacity to "go against" the dough, it will not cause it to rise, and then the dough with all its weight will overcome the leaven.

A priest must always live out a twofold demand: to be in the world and not of it, to understand it and oppose it, to love it and to contradict it. He must always work in the obscurity of faith.

A priest rarely has before his eyes the results of his work. A doctor can see a cure, a lawyer can appreciate the success of his case, an engineer can look at the factory built according to his plans. The priest moves in the mystery of God, in the reality of faith. Josef Loew has well described this dimension in a very fine book whose title itself is a program of life: *Comme s'il voyait l'invisible* ("As though he saw the invisible"). In this vocation to heroism and to the constant exercise of faith, there is a call to a suffering and a struggle inseparable from the very nature of the task to be accomplished. The priest who shares the unique and eternal priesthood has accepted a ministry which finds its wellsprings in the heart of God, and which follows laws transcending our human wisdom.

But if there is a paradox inherent in the priesthood as such, there are today many problems peculiar to our own times. These arise as a result of a whole series of questions, theological, pastoral, sociological and anthropological. The priest is confronted with the problem of identity.

THE PLACE OF PRIESTS

The most striking characteristic of the present-day situation is without doubt the fact that many of our priests are experiencing an increased difficulty in finding their true place in the world, and even in the church.

In today's world, especially in the Western world because it has become dechristianized and progressively deprived of a sense of the sacred, priests are feeling more and more like strangers. Many of them resent this deeply. The difficulty of their task frightens and even discourages them. They attempt to dialogue but men have no regard for the service they offer, or wish no longer to have need of it. They seek to make contact, but are brought up short by the ambiguity of the world. They experience within their own depths the paradox of their mission: to be at the heart of the world those who are set apart for the service of the gospel.

What is the place of the priest in the church of today? Some priests have said that, given the accent placed upon the bishops and the lay people, it seems as though they were forgotten at the council. The attention given to the laity, especially, forces them to question their own specific role in the church. All the faithful are called to be priests, kings and prophets of Christ. All the members of the people of God must be apostles and missionaries. Except for the sacramental ministry, what is unique about a priest?

THE YOUNGER GENERATION

These questions are the concern of every priest, but it is particularly the problems of the younger generations of priests which deserve attention.

Without a doubt there has always been conflict between the generations, but today because of the rapid pace of change in the world this conflict is aggravated. It is at the heart of the "authority-obedience" tension which can be seen in every aspect of life. How many parents complain of this tension and are distraught by it?

The younger generation has its own ways of thinking and acting. They are extremely sensitive to certain values, and allergic to others. They reject a certain image of the conventional Christian, and want no part of a Christianity of repose, conformism and legalism. They are simply not attracted by a religion more preoccupied with avoiding evil than doing good, more anxious to catalogue and draw up an abstract list of sins than to impart a sense of positive love, the spirit of the gospel, and the freedom of the children of God.

These young people, young priests included, feel hobbled by purely disciplinary laws which they look upon as arbitrary. They wish that Christians be no longer insensible to the abuses and injustices of this world, withdrawing into a self-enclosed piety, and restricted to the realm of cult and the sacred. They see no point to a religion which is a stranger to man, and they desire to build a new world more human and true.

These rejections go hand in hand with an openness to positive values. There is a profound sensitivity to all that touches upon respect for the human person and his inalienable rights. There is a reverence for all that concerns conscience and liberty, including the freedom to be wrong, as a condition for an authentic search. They proclaim a style of life and of human relations which is simple and true, free from outdated, hypocritical or simply anachronistic structures. They desire to live more in step with a modern world which cannot accept in its daily life those customs, clothes, titles, laws of etiquette and social amenities which date from former times, and which do not mean anything today either in life or, *a fortiori,* in the world of the arts.

Younger priests, along with the rest of their generation, wish to have frank and open dialogue with authority, not for the purpose of avoiding obedience, but to make obedience a full and adult collaboration. They desire a pastoral and apostolic effort fully adapted to the new sociological reality. There is also a search for Christian communities that are humanly true, where Christians may learn not only how to pray together, but also to unite apostolic and human efforts for the good of men.

Some young priests aspire to apostolic work which is truly daring and novel, and they dream of going out and living fully in the world, there to earn their bread. They are looking too for a renewed catechesis which will reach the man of today. More than one among them appreciate the positive value of marriage and family to such a degree that they could wish that the priesthood be linked to celibacy by way of choice.

We could go on at great length in describing the phenomenology of this rising generation, and filling in many details. But it is sufficient for our purposes to have sketched out the general aspect of the reality and be able to introduce the question: what is the fundamental attitude we should have toward this new situation?

TO UNDERSTAND IN CONTEXT

First, it seems to me, we should not believe we have reached the end of the world. We are at the end of *a* world, but that is a far different thing. It is most important to realize that the phenomenon we have just sketched is universal. We see it in our own ranks, but also we see it everywhere; it forms a part of the climate of our time. The bishop of today, having recognized and situated this tension, must be, more than ever before, the living link between the generations. Even at the risk of seeming too progressive to the older generations or too fearful in the judgment of the young, he must join within himself the past and the future, the tradition to be safeguarded and the progress to be made. This means that we must have a living and serene faith in the Holy Spirit at work in the church yesterday, today and tomorrow.

Since he is the leader of the whole presbytery, the bishop must be, like St. Paul, "in the debt of all men." He is indebted to every generation, the older people as well as the younger. His role is to unite and bind them together, transcending their divergences within the very mystery of the priestly plenitude, seen as never before as a mission to serve the people of God. It is with this vision, and faithful to the fundamental dynamism of his proper function, that the bishop must train all his priests, unifying their diversity of opinions and pastoral tasks.

He should ask of the older priests that they keep their souls young: a sign of a successful spiritual life. Their joy and optimism is the most beautiful gift they can give to their younger brothers about to take over leadership in the church. It is important to note here that there are many priests, some of them quite advanced in age, who have accomplished this effort at adaptation admirably. The bishop must remind the younger priests that the world was not born with them, nor will it die with us. They should be

113

encouraged to have gratitude and respect for those who have preceded them in the field of the Lord. Are we not all the heirs of those who, before us—in another context and with the limitations of their era—gave their best, and awakened the priestly vocations of those who follow them? We must foster pride in our "forefathers in the faith" (Eastern liturgy). It would be a frightful lack in us if we were to forget all that we owe to the great men who have preceded us. To speak only of our own country, Belgium, and to mention only those who are already asleep in the Lord, there come to mind names such as Mercier, Lebbe, Lambert, Beaudouin, Picard, Cardijn, and how many leaders in the theological and philosophical schools at Louvain. These men have proved themselves, and the newer generations still draw on their credit. With the grace of God these younger generations will also produce pioneers and saints, although of a different type: let us put that much confidence in them.

FACING THE FUTURE

The tendencies which animate the younger generations are expressed sometimes in formulas which are unacceptable, and which reflect "growing pains" and a lack of maturity. But a certain excess in the manner of speaking found in some types of literature should not prevent us from grasping the vast undercurrent of renewal present there, and of evaluating its truth.

Reactions against the status quo, structural sclerosis and conformism contain, in a latent way, an appeal for a Christianity lived out with greater truth and courage.

Whatever awakens us to an active, mature and loyal coresponsibility is a grace for the church. The fact that we are called to be guardians of tradition does not mean that we are dedicated to immobility. Authentic tradition ought ceaselessly to free us from purely human traditions, and provide us with fixed navigational points. We are on the march toward the future "until he comes." As we await the return of the Master, we must press forward to meet him. He does not ask us to wrap the past in an aura of perfection. Jesus said that anyone who would go with him must press on without looking back, leaving the dead to bury the dead. The attitude of a Christian is eschatologically oriented: toward the kingdom which is at once already present and still coming.

In God, and because of him, we are men of today and tomorrow. Our apostolate is one with the virtue of hope, and is its practical expression. This fundamental attitude of openness allows us to initiate dialogue and to receive the necessary complementarity deriving from the truth of others.

BASIC VERITIES

Having stepped inside, as it were, and understood with sympathy all that is legitimate in the summons and impatience of the younger generations, we should now speak to them of certain vital truths which run the risk of being obscured because of unilateral insistence upon other values. We should have a sense for "things that exist together," to use an expression of Claudel's. For truths to be truthful, they have need of their harmonic counterpositions: their

115

power derives from their interior balance and integrated equilibrium. As Henri de Lubac once said, "One truth balances another, not by diminishing its force, but by putting it into context."

A Sense of God. The younger generation have a profound sense of man, and this is a great asset. However, they could be tempted to be not quite so open to a sense of God. They love Christ, he who was "a man for others." But they must understand that Christ was a man for others, a man at the service of others, because he was a man at one with the Father. He came in order to do the will of the Father, to "be busy with his Father's affairs," to "tell us of the Father," to teach us the "Our Father." And when on the evening of Holy Thursday, at the hour of the paschal sacrifice, he prepared to leave his disciples, "loving them unto the end" he said to them, "Come now, let us go, that the world might know that I love the Father." Christ is completely given to men because he is completely given over to his Father.

Younger people today may be tempted to forget all this, if they do not discover for themselves the primacy of God, the need for the prayer of adoration, and a sense of contemplation amid the hubbub of daily life. If an apostle does not realize the value of a silence filled with God, his activities will be philanthropic, noble social work, but they will not be a Christian apostolate, the extension of the unique priesthood of Christ.

The depth of his personal union with God remains, for the priest, the fundamental guarantee of his own joy, and of the fruitfulness of his ministry. Union with Christ modifies

116

every aspect of his life, and a priest must have a living awareness of this relationship, which is the very heart of his priesthood. A priest is not primarily—as a whole block of modern literature continues to repeat—at the service of the community which has need of his human resources. A priest is at the service of Jesus Christ who has need of him in order to call the community to a life of faith, to assemble them around the eucharistic table, to bring them to the Father, and to send them out on their mission in the world.

We have need of priests who know how to pray, and can teach others to pray. Religion is not a sort of "spiritual Red Cross," it is communion with God, and in God, a communion with others. There are Christian men and women deeply committed to living out their Christianity who are sometimes surprised to see their shepherds so attentive to the world and its demands, that they seem to have no time to listen when anyone asks them for help in the life of prayer, in a living spirit of faith, a more optimistic hope, or deeper love—briefly, when someone asks for guidance in those realms which pertain to the life of the Spirit. This life will always be the very soul of the priestly ministry, something which must be possessed before it can be shared. And in a very special way, it is in their personal love for Christ that priests will find a motivation to live out their consecrated celibacy.

A Sense of the Church. Our younger people must also have a living and affectionate love for the church. Too often one hears a criticism of the church which is pitiless. It is too easily forgotten that, even if men are what they are and if every human structure is deficient and falls short of the ideal, Christ himself is always present and active within the heart of his church which is and will remain "our mother, the holy church." People willingly recall the errors and abuses committed by men of the church, and point out how many great theologians today were but yesterday the objects of suspicion. This is true, but we must not block from our view the nobility of soul and the depth with which these same theologians knew how to accept silence and suffer for and from the church. Someone like Henri de Lubac could write unforgettable passages about the mystery of the church during the very time that he was beset by difficulties and obstacles arising from that church.[1]

Sad to say, there are priests who have left the church because they were too bruised by its structures. The church seemed to them too human to be a sacrament of God. But has not the church from the very beginnings of its history been made up of men of flesh and blood, beset with weakness and misery just like the rest of us? From the pope down to the least of us, do we not all say the *confiteor* and strike our breast?

Have not these priests read the gospel? Look at the stuff the apostles were made of. Who was this son of Jonas called Peter, the rock? A weak man, inconsistent with himself, to whom Jesus said one day, "Get behind me, satan!" —a man who denied his master, and left him to die on Calvary. Peter, the leader of the church, who after the Council of Jerusalem gave in to the pressure of the judaizers to such a degree that Paul had to contradict him to his face. All of this pertains to that side of Peter which is shadow and weakness. But Peter has another aspect,

1. Cf. H. de Lubac, *The Splendour of the Church,* New York, 1956, especially chapter 8, "Our Temptations Concerning the Church."

where there is light and inner truth. He was the first to confess "the Christ, the Son of the living God." It was he who dared to walk on the water, and it was Peter who stood before the crowd on the morning of Pentecost, an unshakable witness to the resurrection, and who finally died witnessing to his faith.

This is the kind of human stuff that Christ uses to form the hierarchy of his church. No one should be surprised if God is pleased to take such poor instruments as we are and do great, even very great things. Then too, "Consider your own call, brothers. When you were called, how many of you were wise in the ordinary sense of the word, how many were influential people, or came from noble families? No, it was to shame the wise that God chose what is foolish by human reckoning, and to shame what is strong that he chose what is weak by human reckoning" (1 Cor. 1, 26–27).

No amount of disappointment can be a legitimate excuse for quitting our mother the church. It is to this mother even today that humanity owes what is best in itself. The church and those who remain faithful to her have, through the centuries, carried the torch of the gospel, thus enabling others at times to see better than we do by its light.

A Sense of Progress. Our young priests must have a delicate sense of their pastoral responsibilities concerning the faithful confided to their care. Always to surprise them, always to be right up to the minute, thoughtlessly to upset age-old customs, to deprive people of a way of thinking and supply nothing in its stead—these are the ways we become a stumbling block causing others to fall away.

A shepherd must advance at the pace of his flock, and be

on the lookout that each of those for whom he is responsible does not wander from the path. If he is a good shepherd, he will know how to act with speed and energy when the situation requires it. But he will also know how to bide his time, awaiting the right moment, giving time a chance to act, having the patience of a good educator, bringing others along step by step rather than needlessly upsetting them. He must take all the faithful into account, including those who are not very progressive, as a mother does with her children. He must constantly remind himself that the faithful of today are not those described by the predictions for 1980! Is this not simply to be realistic? And such realism demands patience and real virtue: it is a sign of a weak man to insist on realizing everything right now, no matter whom it upsets. Patience respects the laws of life. It requires real strength to progress step by step serenely, having a good sense of what is possible, able to move at the pace of others and to remain in community.

A priest must always be aware of how those who listen to him are likely to understand him, and how they may react to a statement or the presentation of a paradox. This is a very important aspect of pastoral love: we are not the messengers of our own ideas, we are called to pass on faithfully the unique message of Christ, and to strive to see that it is understood. We are humble servants of a word greater than we are, and which will one day be our judge. We must present this word in such a way that every degree of intelligence can receive it, so that the people of God may live by this message, feed on it, and grow until we all attain to the "perfect Man, to the measure of the stature of the fullness of Christ" (Eph. 4, 13).

The Practice of Priestly Coresponsibility

Let us consider now the practice of coresponsibility within the life of priests. Coresponsibility is at the very heart of the priestly mission because it is at the heart of the church's mission. Collegiality conditions this mission, since it is the collegial church which is sent out to the world. Thus coresponsibility is at the heart of the relation between the bishop and the priests, between the priests themselves, and between the priests and lay people. Let us consider each of these in turn.

THE PRIESTS AND THE BISHOP

The council reinstated concelebrated Mass which, in recent centuries, had been seen only at ordination ceremonies. Concelebration achieves its full meaning when the priests are around the altar with their bishop: there the unity of the presbyterate is affirmed.

Priests are not individuals juxtaposed one with another, they are sharers in a unique priesthood, the priesthood of Christ, communicated to them by the bishop. They participate in a mystery of communion which achieves visible expression in the common celebration of the eucharistic sacrifice. This same mystery lived out in the liturgy extends from the altar to include all the pastoral activity which radiates through the diocese from the bishop. The pastoral activity of all finds its full meaning when it becomes a sort of "pastoral concelebration" deriving its reality from the eucharistic concelebration.

121

During the ceremony at ordination, there is a point which dramatically highlights the deep union between the priests and their bishop. As the bishop is about to impose his hands on those he is to ordain, all the other priests present at the ceremony come and form a circle around the bishop and also impose their hands. This gesture does not enter into the essence of the sacrament, but its symbolic force is eloquent. We must continue this language of the liturgy in our daily activities, translating into act the logic of its symbol.

The reality of the presbyterate forms an adequate basis on which to construct a theology of the priesthood. If one parts from this basis, he sets out on a path that leads nowhere. If we consider the priest as isolated, we will find it impossible to discern his role and to determine the priestly value of his functions. We can never forget that the priest is not a self-enclosed unit. The unit which we must consider is the presbyterate which, along with the bishop, assumes responsibility for the pastoral charge of the diocese. A diversity of roles and functions is inherent in the very constitution of the ecclesial ministry. The whole presbytery has the responsibility to maintain the church in an attitude of prayer, worship, love and mission.

The priesthood is a reality which is one and manifold: it is something to be lived out together. We are all familiar with this text of St. Paul describing the mystery of the "one and the many" in the church:

Just as each of our bodies has several parts and each part has a separate function, so all of us, in union with Christ, form one body, and as parts of it we belong to each other. Our gifts differ according to the grace given us. If your gift is prophecy, then use it as your faith suggests; if administration, then use it for administration; if teaching then use it for teaching. Let the preachers deliver sermons, the almsgivers give freely, the officials be diligent, and those who do work of mercy do them cheerfully (Rom. 12, 4–8).

The "Two Clergies." When we speak of the relationship between the priests and the bishop, there is a distinction to be made between those priests dedicated directly to the service of the diocese and religious priests who have their own proper obligations. Without entering here into details or refinements, let us note that the council foresees a closer collaboration between these two bodies of priests within a context of a common pastoral effort; and it has established certain pastoral norms in this regard. The council also contributed to reducing, at the doctrinal level, the once classic opposition which made the diocesan priests the priests of the bishop, and the religious priests the priests of the pope. This opposition is now out of date; the council has clearly accentuated the fact that all priests pertain to the universal body of bishops. It was made manifest that every priest is a *cooperator ordinis nostri,* a co-worker with the whole episcopal order at the head and heart of which is the pope. Every priest pertains, in varying ways, to the over-all unity of the episcopacy. Ordination, which establishes a bond between the priest and the bishop of a particular church, binds him indissolubly through this bishop to the episcopacy to the world. Therein are found the roots of priestly coresponsibility in its relation to the whole church.

The council, then, accentuates the coresponsibility of these "two clergies" within the heart of the universal church as well as within each particular church. Among the encouraging signs of our times, we rejoice to see this collab-

123

oration achieve an institutional expression insofar as this is possible at the moment. This is the time for uniting spirits and hearts in a work which is more and more integrated, and within which religious priests rediscover the charismatic intuition of their own vocation. They are learning once again to esteem the unique value of this vocation, and by that very fact, to situate it within the pastoral activity of the bishop while making their particular and irreplaceable contribution. We are in this regard, at the very beginning stages, but the direction is well taken.

The Senate of Priests. Presbyterial collegiality received a new impulse at the council, by the creation of the senate of priests, a body which, from now on, will form an integral part of diocesan life. This senate was described in the motu proprio of August 6, 1966, which served to render explicit the desire expressed by the fathers at the council:

> There should be a council of priests in each diocese, according to a manner and form established by the bishop. It will be a group or senate of priests, representing the whole presbyterate, who through their advice can effectively help the bishop in the government of the diocese. In this council the bishop should listen to his priests, consult them and talk to them about things pertaining to pastoral needs and the good of the diocese.

This council has a consultative function and must be located within the ensemble of the various councils of the bishop: the episcopal council, the council of deans and the diocesan pastoral council, to list but the principal examples. This is not the place to give a precise description of the functions pertaining to the senate of priests, since it is an area still being researched. However, we can say that this senate, whose structure and functions will one day receive greater determination from canon law, represents the presbyterate as such with a view to aiding the bishop in the government of the diocese.

It is a striking fact that the constitutive texts pertaining to the senate of priests stress so strongly its representative character, while the manner of appointing members—by the bishop or not, in whole or in part—is left to the discretion of the bishop. A presbyterial council would not answer to its purpose if it did not express, insofar as this is possible, the principal functions exercised within the apostolic ministry. It is to be remarked also that this senate functions as a whole: from the moment of their appointment the members become part of a presbyterate, and assume a collective responsibility.

But it would be an impoverished and false concept of this senate which would see in each member nothing more than the representative of his group, the messenger of those whom he represents and to whom he must refer for every important decision. Once he is elected or appointed, a member of the priestly senate becomes a part of a whole, and must exercise global coresponsibility.

The council wished that this senate be a structure fostering dialogue between the bishop and the priests; it should tend to intensify their collaboration and facilitate their mutual relations. One of the greatest desires on the part of priests throughout the world is to have more real contact with their bishop, real dialogue, and greater common pastoral coresponsibility.

This same desire has been expressed at every level of the church. Lay people also wish to have better contact and more real collaboration with their priests. In order to respond to this desire, all of those responsible for the pastoral effort in the diocese must assume their share of spiritual paternity. If the bishop should be the "image of the Father" for his priests and his people, then all his immediate collaborators must share in this duty. The vicars general, the deans, the pastors, each according to his proper function, must participate in this episcopal paternity, and as it were multiply it. Whatever contributes to decentralization and a fully shared responsibility will contribute to genuine relations, as well as contacts which are truly human and friendly. But these relationships must be true, open, sincere and transcend administrative and other types of formalism.

On the other hand, we must be on guard that this senate of priests, born of the desire to structure and solidify dialogue between the bishop and the priests, does not prove false to itself and become a substitute for individual contact. Experience will help to harmonize this twofold demand of individual and collective contact: these should be mutually complementary.

Conditions for Dialogue. For the dialogue between priests and bishops to be a success, there are, as is the case for any dialogue, certain prerequisites.

It must be, on the part of all engaged in it, a true dialogue.

It must conform to the norms of respect, loyalty, sincerity and love.

It must transpire above and beyond juridicism, and be

established in a Christian atmosphere of communion.

Now let us explain these prerequisites.

True Dialogue. As a matter of fact, though the word "dialogue" is on everyone's lips today, true dialogue is extremely rare.

But what is a dialogue? Many of our dialogues are, unfortunately, little more than a tiring interchange of monologue. True dialogue is first and foremost a listening to the other, and we all know that it is more difficult to listen than to speak. Few people really listen to others. Few people realize that they have two ears and only one mouth; that nature itself seems to invite us to listen twice as much as we speak.

We must listen to another, not simply out of courtesy, or for the pleasure of hearing his voice, but in order to be affected and to be enriched by contact with him. To listen to another is, so to speak, to go to his school with the conviction that he has something to give me. It is to put one's confidence in a man, awakening in him a sense of his own liberty, and by that very fact opening him to the exchange of true dialogue.

Without that mutual exchange which takes place in an atmosphere of mutual listening, there is no true relationship between men. Even the service which one wishes to render falls short of its ultimate goal in such a situation and inevitably degenerates into a paternalism which is nothing other than a caricature of true love. Instead of fostering the freedom of a man, it binds him, consciously or unconsciously, in submission to his "benefactor."

127

Paternalism is the perversion of paternal love. It is the effort of a father to bind the child to himself, and hold him in a state of minority; to keep him as a possession rather than to aid him in arriving himself at the autonomy of a true adult. Paternalism is the very opposite of that profound expression of Louis Lavelle: "The greatest thing that we can do for others is not to communicate to them our riches, but to reveal to them their own."

A Constructive Dialogue. It is perfectly normal that there be public opinion in the church, and normal too that it express itself. Pius XII, recognizing its right to existence, once said:

> No one should be surprised at this fact, except those who do not know the church, or know it fully. For the church is a living body, and there would be something lacking to its life if public opinion were absent, and the blame for this absence would be shared by both pastors and the faithful.[2]

Liberty of public opinion within the church is a right, but it implies the responsibility of exercising it in faith and charity. We must guard ourselves against both mute servility and uncontrolled criticism.

Public opinion must express itself in accord with the laws of maturity, of fair play, of discretion, of respect for the rules of the game, and with a sense of communal responsibility. To express one's thought is not the same as gathering a crowd, or looking for success with the audience; it is rather to give the best of oneself for the benefit of all, with the view toward positive collaboration.

2. Address to Journalists, October 27, 1957.

The senate of priests will be fruitful to the degree that it is a common effort, dedicated to analyzing problems and searching together for solutions. It is not difficult to draw up a list of things that should not be, or to compose a catalogue of complaints. It is more difficult to point out true remedies, to offer ideas that are balanced, and to take account of all the factors involved. Backroom strategies are many. But it is not sufficient to criticize: we must build. Someone once said that the world has greater need of masons than of architects. Without denying the usefulness of the latter, we must admit that the world does not abound with people who know how to construct a building brick by brick, slowly and methodically.

Active participation on the part of the collaborators in the working out of pastoral decisions is by that very fact— and this consideration should be borne in mind—the greatest guarantee that the decision will be carried out. The process by which a decision is arrived at is as important as the decision itself. Modern democracy is engaged precisely in the effort to determine and respect the laws of this process. There is no questioning here of authority, just the contrary. Authority is not safeguarded by taking refuge in silence or in mystery, though of course there must be discretion exercised in the discussion of personalities.

For the bishop himself this convergence of the efforts of all with a view to discovering the common good is a very precious thing. He well knows how difficult it is to assess, all by himself, all the factors of a situation. As beneficiary of the experience of all, and enlightened by them, his own vision and insight will grow. The bishop's grace of state, guaranteed to him by God in virtue of his consecration, is operative as he listens to others. Every one of his priests owes to the bishop, and through him to all, the very best of his own priestly riches.

Beyond Juridicism. The council, and the motu proprio which rendered its thought more precise, gave the senate of priests the status of a consultative, not a deliberative, body. The bishop is told to consult his priests with the view toward governing the people of God confided to the care of all. The full right of making ultimate decisions rests with the bishop. However, this status can become a temptation for both the bishop and the priests. If the bishop does not take his role seriously, he will go through the motions of listening, and then go on his way. If the priests do not take their role seriously, they could minimize the possibilities of these regular meetings under the pretext that they "have no rights."

Dialogue transpires in a realm beyond juridic relationships. What the bishop desires to discover in his priests is not primarily obedience, but a sharing in theological hope. We ought to apply here, with the obvious modifications, that which will be said in Chapter VIII, concerning authority and obedience in the religious life. The basis of common pastoral effort, as well as the basis for any friendship, must be *"idem velle et idem nolle"* ("to will and not will the same things"). The priest must offer the bishop a joyous, relaxed and committed collaboration. And let us not forget the role of humor: that precious gift which keeps things in proportion, oneself as well as others, and which is one of the most subtle and precious gifts of the Holy Spirit, even if it does not figure in the official lists.

130

Priests among Themselves. Priestly coresponsibility is not restricted to the relationships between the priests and the bishop, but must be exercised also in the relationships that priests have among themselves. On the juridical level this involves some revisions to be incorporated within the new canon law.

We are thinking in particular, for example, of the relationship between pastors and curates. Canonically speaking, the pastor is everything, and the curates are meant to help carry out his plan: there is no true coresponsibility. In our existing legislation, curates have no status and no direct responsibility. This is a situation which opposes the awakening and the development of their personality as much as it blocks the realization of any efficacious pastoral activity.

By right, it is the pastor alone who makes decisions. He holds all the power in a monarchical situation which leads to a hybrid regime, with which we are all too familiar, and which could be called a regime of "singular responsibility and parallel activity." As he carries out the duties which concern him, the curate, almost by the nature of the situation, is led to create little states within the state, small groupings more or less integrated within the parish life. The disadvantages of such a system were, perhaps, not so evident in a social context different from ours, when the parish objectives were static and quite limited. At the moment, when religious sociology has opened up so many pastoral possibilities, and when theology and the liturgy now require the effort of all, it has become impossible to maintain an individualistic manner of acting in which each man is unaware of the activities of the others.

Canon law has as yet not utilized the notion of the collegiality of the priesthood. It is familiar only with responsi-

131

bility discharged on a strictly individual level. But we must rediscover the meaning of priestly collegiality, especially in those areas where priests come in constant contact with one another, that is to say, on the level of local or parochial teams.

The priestly ministry must become a responsibility carried by all, in which all the priests involved have a real part in the pastoral work. Priests must feel that they are integrated in the parish, aware of everything that concerns it. They must know the objectives to be accomplished and the means to be used, so that they can locate their personal contribution within the common effort. This supposes that they all have true responsibility and that there is real discussion utilizing the initiatives, energies and abilities of all.

No one is questioning the existence of a leader, of someone ultimately responsible. What is under discussion is the very nature of his function, and thus his role and place. The problem is not primarily one of safeguarding unity of command, it is much more profound than that. The fundamental role of the leader is to make collegiality possible. He is its guarantee. He is there primarily so that each member may be part of a whole, and thus assume full responsibility within and toward a common effort. The role of the one in charge is not that of making a "personal" decision after having taken the advice of others into account. For in that case it would still be "his" decision. His role is rather to make it possible, insofar as this depends upon him, for there to be a common decision which commits each member to the decision, in such a way that they are solidly behind it and willing to accept all the consequences of what has been decided together. A true leader, ultimately responsible for the pastoral work of a locale, will find his place when he has succeeded in helping the others find theirs.

While awaiting canon law to formulate the norms, priests should try various experiments in collegiality in union with the authority of the diocese. Practical rules of common action will emerge more readily when there is active collaboration on the part of all.

But beyond these juridical readjustments, as important as they may be, we should look at the immense possibilities on the spiritual level for priestly collegiality. Friendship between priests and the mutual support which they can give to one another are inestimable graces for the priests themselves, and for their apostolic activities. The isolation which ecclesiastical celibacy entails should, no doubt, be balanced by a strong interior life and a genuine asceticism, but it should also be lived out within an atmosphere of affectionate and brotherly communion which grows with the passage of years because of an intimate sharing of a common ideal with others. We must resolutely leave behind the era of individualism and isolation, and develop those things which lead to a sense of community.

Seminary education as it has been previously conceived has left each of us with gaps to be filled. The newer generations of priests must learn from the beginning how to live and work as a team. They must experience solidarity and be introduced into a sense of coresponsibility which they can put into practice for the rest of their lives. It is legitimate for some to live out this reality by expressing it in a common life. Not all will necessarily feel themselves called to live this way, but all must understand that they must learn the meaning of shared responsibility in a work which is common to all of us. Nearly everywhere throughout the world, research is going on to elaborate this pedagogy proper to our time. We are trying, for our part, to experiment in this direction at the John XXIII Seminary at Louvain. It is still too soon to attempt to describe it. It must be left to grow and mature, and other seminaries inspired by Vatican II must also grow so that we can share our experiences for the benefit of all. Priestly coresponsibility will not happen just by itself, it will be the responsibility of coming generations to bring it to life throughout the whole church.

Priests and Lay People. But this priestly coresponsibility is not limited only to the priesthood, it must extend to include the relationship between the priests and the laity. We can hardly do more than touch upon this subject here, but it must be said that there is a certain type of spiritual literature which must be brought up to date in this regard.

At times the role of the priest as "mediator" between God and men was accentuated to the detriment of the mediating role of the whole church. Sometimes there has been too much insistence on a definition of the priest as "another Christ," forgetting that the layman also, because of his baptism, can and ought to say with St. Paul, "It is no longer I who live, Christ lives in me." We cannot make this definition the specific characteristic of the priesthood.

Yet, the priest has an incomparable mission to fulfill within the church because he shares in a particular way in the role of Christ as head of the mystical body. It is in this context that his function is situated. It pertains to him to build the Christian community, and to animate it. He is the head and heart giving life to the body. His role is to give life to the community of believers, feeding them with the

134

word of God and the eucharist, making them aware of their mission to evangelize and humanize the world.

It is for him to approach, directly or indirectly, every baptized person, revealing to them their total apostolic vocation, and helping them to find their fields of action while encouraging their efforts. In a special way, his is the task of coordinating the efforts of all, and drawing out all the potential of the life of the Christian laity within the people of God, so that each person contributes his own charisms for the building up of the church.

In the words of Henri Denis, we must recognize the work of the priest as being "interior to the work of the whole church." We must understand that there is no "hierarchical priesthood which is not ordered to the priesthood of the people of God."

VI.

The Coresponsibility of Theologians

Since coresponsibility is becoming more characteristic of the life of the church, it is to be expected that it receive the same prominence among theologians. The collaboration of theologians cannot be compared with the collaboration implied in episcopal collegiality, for theological study, in the very nature of its own dynamics, takes place at the level of scientific research, though its contribution to the good of the whole Christian body is considerable. We are touching here on a very delicate point, and one which directly concerns those conditions necessary for the full realization of the council.

Intercommunication of ideas governs the pastoral activity of tomorrow. This kind of exchange is indispensable for the enrichment of theology itself, and it is indispensable as well for the true catholicity of the church on the doctrinal level. Paul VI told the theologians:

Deprived of theology's efforts, the magisterium would lack the tools it needs to weld the Christian community into a unified con-

136

cert of thought and action, a community thinking and living according to Christ's precepts and norms.[1]

Unity of faith is consistent with a certain theological pluralism, just as the same worship of adoration is expressed through diverse liturgies: "There are many rooms in my father's house." It is impossible to reduce all of theological thought to but one of its expressions, to the teaching of just one doctor, even if it be St. Thomas himself, as the council clearly noted when this saint's eminent place within the thought of the church was discussed.

Speaking to a meeting of Thomists in Rome, Paul VI said concerning St. Thomas:

The magisterium of the church did not intend to make of him an exclusive master, neither imposing every one of his theses, nor excluding legitimate diversity of schools or theological systems, much less prohibiting just freedom of research.[2]

This rejection of a theological monopoly corresponds to the imperfection inherent in our formulas of faith. As the Belgium episcopacy wrote in its collective letter, "Our Faith in Jesus Christ":

The concepts that we use, the figures of our imagination, the symbols or comparisons to which we have recourse, all of these are not God, though they can lead us to God without error provided that we ceaselessly correct the imperfections of our manner of speaking and thinking. For God is "utterly Other" than the creature, and no human expression can encompass him. He always remains greater than our statements about him and the conceptual

1. Address to International Congress on the Theology of Vatican II, October 1, 1966.
2. Allocution to Sixth International Thomistic Congress, September 10, 1965.

array which we need in order to speak of him, or receive his revelation. Even the revelation which comes from the lips of Jesus Christ is not identical with Christ himself. Thus we always tend by faith toward God through the formulas which we do not know how to surmount, and which we must always understand more deeply and render more intelligible to contemporaneous thought. But of necessity, in order to reach God himself in authentic ways, we must go beyond these formulas.

In recognizing the principle that unity is not uniformity, we do not become estranged from one another, but rather meet at a deeper level of unity, brought to a more central common denominator which has been freed of many of its human accretions. To identify orthodoxy with one theological school of thought is to misunderstand the height, depth and immensity of God's mysteries.

In order to experience the importance and gravity of this necessary catholicity of thought it is sufficient to learn the lesson given by the council.

The Experience of the Council

Let us recall for a moment the doctrinal preparatory work for the council. A group of theologians received the commission to prepare the conciliar schemas. The central commission, composed of about 100 cardinals, bishops and religious superiors, received the mandate to examine these schemas. During the meetings of this central committee, the schemas underwent a severe criticism on the part of certain cardinals and bishops. At these meetings the critics continually repeated that these preparatory schemas corresponded neither to the actual state of the problem, nor to the present state of theology. However, these preliminary warnings were without effect, and the schemas were presented to the council. There they underwent a trial by fire. We all know the result: the great majority of the conciliar fathers pronounced their *"non placet"* and sent the initial schemas back to be redone.

It is worthwhile reflecting on this page of recent history and upon the deficiencies it revealed. What appeared in the full light of day was a divergence between two theological outlooks, and consequently, the rejection of a certain defined orthodoxy monopolized up to that point by a restricted group of theologians all of whom shared the same tendencies. What the council rejected was not only a group of texts which were considered too juridical and insufficiently pastoral. Beyond the rejected schemas there lay a theological outlook which was judged to be too narrow, too much "of the school," and too divorced from reality.

Bishop G. Philips has well described the typology of the two theological temperaments that met at the council. Of one group he writes:

They treat truth as a monolithic thing, and do not always distinguish the various levels of certitude because they are preoccupied above all with keeping the truth safe from danger. Sometimes because they lack background, they confuse tradition with opinions that were current during recent centuries, or even with their own habitual concepts, insufficiently controlled by contact with others. This results in their considering as novelties, opinions which pertain to a tradition which is older and more authentic, but somewhat obliterated. Thus they easily become suspicious and patronizing, and their teaching takes on a polemic and negative character.

139

He describes the other group as follows:

> Convinced that its view of truth is not identical in all its forms with the truth itself, this group knows full well that our intellectual categories view truth and obtain it really, but cannot give it adequate expression. They possess, moreover, a sense of history. And while they consider every definition sanctioned by the church to be true in itself, they believe, nevertheless, that these can be made clearer and expressed more lucidly. One council can perfect the definition of its predecessor, for example, by showing more clearly how a solemn but partial teaching fits within the whole of a complex doctrine.[3]

All of this pertains to the realm of conceptualization. But there is also here something deeper. Up to the eve of the council, the orthodoxy of any affirmation was judged and classified by a group of theologians who tended to identify certain of their own opinions with the intrinsic demands of faith. This was serious, first of all, because it was a practical misunderstanding of legitimate pluralism within certain limits, as well as the necessary distinction to be made between affirmations which directly touch upon faith and others which were but theological conclusions. In regard to legitimate pluralism, Paul VI has said:

> In matters so difficult and so removed from the realm of common experience, some reasonable differences of opinion are perfectly compatible with the unity of faith and with fidelity toward the teachings and guidelines of the magisterium. These differences of opinion should cause no surprise. In fact, they should be considered quite useful. For they serve as an impetus to deeper and more accurate analysis of one's line of reasoning; and sincere, well-grounded discussions bring the full truth to light at last.[4]

3. *Nouvelle revue théologique* (1963), pp. 228–229.
4. Address to International Congress on the Theology of Vatican II.

What added to the gravity of the situation was the fact that some of the theses proposed by those who wished to monopolize orthodoxy were, as a matter of fact, questionable or, at least, to be treated with caution. The council, by an impressive majority, left these theses to one side. To take full account of the import of these rejections, it suffices to compare certain passages of the initial schemas with the definitive texts voted upon by the council. In Chapter I we have given many examples of this comparison.

The shift from a theology which could be summarily called "of the Roman school" to a theology "of a universal council" was, to an appreciable degree, the work of theological experts who labored on the conciliar commissions, or on their fringe. Their collaboration contributed the wealth of a thought which was large, nuanced and open to the modern view of problems. The whole movement of renewal in the fields of biblical, patristic, dogmatic, moral and liturgical studies thus entered fully into this healthy and varied brewing of ideas. But the contribution was not made without pain. Up to the moment of the council, certain theologians of international reputation were considered suspect. They had accepted this suffering nobly for the sake of the church, preparing by their labor and their pain for the hour when the deepest and fullest truth would be recognized.

This drama of incomprehension was primarily due to the lack of dialogue between the theological schools of the "center" and those of the "periphery." There was a gap between the theologies, and we must objectively admit this gap and avoid it for the future.

The seriousness of such divisions is appreciated when we recall that every governing body is dominated by the vision which animates those who direct it: the Roman curia is no exception to this law. When we speak of the reform of the curia and of necessary internationalization, we generally think of balancing the preponderance of Italian members by the addition of those from elsewhere. Such a preoccupation is fully justified, but, more important than knowing that the head of a congregation be Italian, French, Spanish or Asiatic, one ought to know what his theology is. For, in the words of Proudhon, "at the basis of every political problem, there is a theological problem." It is to be presumed that practical pastoral activity will be influenced by the way one views orthodoxy.

A view of this type dominates practical daily options and is operative when there is a choice to make of men who will be given positions of authority throughout the world. The choice of a bishop is determined, among other things, by the soundness of his doctrine. But who is going to determine this if not those who are themselves modified by their own theological formation? The theology of a papal nuncio is more important than his nationality. If we wish, and correctly so, that solid men be placed at the service of the church, it is very important to know and determine correctly the criteria by which their orthodoxy and soundness of doctrine will be judged.

If the doctrinal vision of those responsible for such decisions is too narrow, their judgments about people cannot but be insufficiently founded, and there is a great risk that men of authentic orthodoxy, whose ideas do not happen to square with those of a given school, will be passed over. We should avoid those kind of dramatic situations as occurred, for instance, in the case of Newman, whom Leo XIII had to make a cardinal in order to establish beyond

142

doubt that his theology was at least as valid as that of his opponents.

What we have just said about ideas which modify the way men govern is particularly applicable to the problem of a retirement age. This is now happily provided for in the motu proprio *Sanctae Ecclesiae*. As a man advances in age it becomes more and more difficult to follow the movement of ideas, and to grasp the exact significance of problems as they arise. This is the price we all pay for the "joy of growing old," to use the phrase of Jacques Leclercq. In today's world, the new problems are not only theological. But, due to the rapid changeover of sociological conditions, there is a new pastoral effort to be continually renewed, watched and adapted, if it is to remain realistic.

Toward a Better Balance

An important change has already been introduced since the end of the council in order to assure a better balance in doctrinal matters: the Congregation of the Holy Office has become the Congregation of the Doctrine of the Faith. Certain procedures have been abolished—no one regrets this—and the number of consultors drawn from outside has been increased. The episcopacy of the world appreciates the fact that they were consulted in regard to a series of doctrinal propositions. This allows, if not for direct meeting and an exchange of views properly so called, at least for greater access to information.

The decree on the reform of the curia which became effective March 1, 1968, provides, in conformity with the motu proprio *Pro Comperto Sane,* for the nomination of seven residential bishops to each curial congregation. This measure will be an important step to the degree that these bishops are able to take an effective part in the deliberations, and an effective and consistent part in determining general theological orientation and consequent decisions: this is the intention of the motu proprio.

A Wish of the Synod

The bishops who assisted at the Roman synod in October 1967 were of the opinion that there is still some progress to be made if we really wish to assure organization and permanent theological collaboration answering to all the present needs. We are all aware that the doctrinal commission of the synod was responsible for synthesizing views and suggestions in doctrinal matters expressed by the bishops who themselves represented the episcopal conferences of the world. This commission formulated the following proposition:

Do the fathers of the synod desire that a theological commission be created, to be composed of men qualified by their wisdom and international reputation, appointed for a specified time, representing both East and West, whose mission would be to offer their services, in complete scientific liberty, to the Holy See and especially to the Congregation of the Doctrine of the Faith, in matters of major doctrinal importance?

The response to this question was impressive: by a vote of 124 favorable to 14 opposed, the episcopacy of the world made known its favorable reply. The 39 *"placet juxta modum"* were concerned with the theological commission's manner of existence, not with the timeliness of its creation. This sounding out of opinion was revealing. If the synod had only produced this one result, its contribution would already have been positive and constructive. We said it was a "sounding out of opinion," because the synod was not called upon to formulate a decision, but to propose a suggestion to papal authority. It would be up to this authority to formulate the solution which it considered best. On the hypothesis that there would be a favorable response, the bishops went on, by a vote of 137 to 18, to propose the following:

. . . that the names of first-rate theologians be proposed to the Holy See by the episcopal conferences, which, after having contacted the Catholic universities or faculties in their region, consider that there are men in their territory of this stature.

Now all of this was the expression of a wish and a suggestion. There could be no question of defining this commission more precisely. It was not the affair of the synod to articulate the manner which this commission would be related to the doctrinal congregation itself, nor to propose reforms for the directive functions of the congregation. What the fathers of the synod wished to accomplish was to have a group of capable theologians, of worldwide reputation and legitimately diverse theological tendencies, effectively collaborating on a doctrinal level with the supreme magisterium in order to make a contribution at once highly qualified and inspired by a shared, profound love of the church. They were thinking of a commission similar to the biblical commission.

This theological commission seemed to be all the more desirable since too often second-rate theologians, or even variously inspired non-theologians, disturb public opinion in the church with hypotheses that true science could never tolerate. This actualization of coresponsibility on the part of real theologians cannot but be of great benefit to the church. There is, however, one condition which has been foreseen and expressed: this exercise of coresponsibility must take place in an atmosphere of true liberty. Once the limits demanded by the very dignity of the word of God, which is eternal, have been established, there lies open a great field of research where it is recognized that "all the faithful, clerical and lay, possess a lawful freedom of inquiry and of thought, and a freedom to express their minds humbly and courageously about those matters in which they enjoy competence" (*Modern World,* art. 62). Paul VI, after having cited the above passage, went on to say, "It is precisely this lawful freedom which is the foundation of theological progress."[5]

There is another condition as well: theologians must work together with those who are competent in other scientific disciplines. "Through a sharing of resources and points of view, let those who teach in seminaries, colleges and universities try to collaborate with men well versed in the other sciences" (*Modern World,* art. 62). This collaboration on a large scale is not only useful but absolutely necessary for all that concerns the relations between the church and the world.

5. Letter to International Congress on the Theology of Vatican II, September 21, 1966.

Theological Maturity

Of course, doctrinal judgments to which the magisterium totally commits its supreme apostolic authority are infallible, and thus unchangeable. But all the other judgments retain a certain theoretical margin of reformability to a greater or less degree, according to whether or not there is question of a minor and occasional decision or a solemn declaration. Then too, the magisterium does not have the answer for everything. "Let the layman not imagine that his pastors are always such experts, that to every problem which arises, however complicated, they can readily give him a concrete solution, or even that such is their mission" (*ibid.*, art. 43).

The church can and ought to take its time, sometimes quite a long time, before defining its thought on a controversial matter. During this period of discussion and controversy, the role of theologians is especially indispensable. It is very important that they be able to fulfill this role so that a new question can mature and arrive at a state in which the hierarchy of the church may be able to express itself on the subject. It would be dangerous for the very good of the truth to be proposed in all its richness, if the time for maturing were to be omitted or unduly shortened. Time—and thus also patience—is a factor which must also be integrated in the life of the church. As has been quite correctly said, the magisterium is not a sort of press office answering "on the go" all the questions of the day which the world proposes. Rather, the magisterium must engage in a continuous work of explanation, clarification and enriching of the good news. It is at this level that theologians must

147

labor, it is thus that they are permanent and indispensable collaborators in the teaching office of the church.

Theological Complementarity

Theologians should mutually complement one another. Just as in the ancient cathedrals the buttresses were placed against the transverse arches, so theologians work together within the church when they variously accent complementary views. We must join together a concern for unity, doctrinal continuity and the demands of tradition, with a desire for direct contact with the currents of thought in our modern world. The complementarity of various points of view is of benefit to the church and of profit for all. Theology lives out its life within the church, and the church is at one and the same time a reality of the past, an actuality of the present, and an openness for the future. In this sense the church itself is both "memory and prophecy."

However, today the problems that we face reach across oceans and are discussed at the same time in the most varied contexts. That is why, more than ever before, there must be a coordination of research and a vast exchange of information.

We need the converging effort of our theologians in order to establish a doctrinal foundation for the pastoral efforts of the faithful. To give but one example, pointed out during a session of the council by the Patriarch Maximos IV, there is great need for theological reflection, dialogue and coresponsibility so that we may see clearly how to interpret ecclesiastical law.

There are many factors which have contributed to the

148

decadence of moral theology during the last few centuries. Placed as it was under the domination of canonists, and drawing more and more upon an abstract casuistry, it lost a necessary and vivifying contact both with the sources of tradition and with the human sciences. Since the beginning of our century many theologians have reacted against this situation by bringing to light the true perspectives of Christian morality.

But then, the interpretation of ecclesiastical laws, striving as it does to bring out their true sense and significance, can only transpire in the light of the gospel message. It must take into account the dimension of history and open itself out to a positive and dynamic vision. We must discover the fundamental value which these laws wished to promote and safeguard, under different forms, throughout the course of the church's history. During the last few centuries, theological manuals, the usual seminary teaching, and confessional practice have accented the negative aspect. Laws were presented as barriers, or as immutable commands relating to precise acts. Sufficient care was not taken to bring out the fundamental values which these laws contain and the virtues they imply. Then also, these laws were often promulgated under pain of mortal sin, and attention was concentrated on an isolated act to avoid (eating meat on Friday) or to perform (mass on Sunday). Thus, in an increasing degree, all these various factors led inevitably to a formalism which was more or less profound, and always dangerous.

Now we must foster open and collaborative theological research in order to discover the positive meaning of these various ecclesiastical laws, as well as the values which should be proposed, and a more exact understanding of the

149

qualification "under pain of mortal sin." This research, situated in the true perspectives of morality, will bring to the whole of Christian life the expression of a correctly existential attitude. The interpretation of the law of abstinence as it is now presented is a good typical example. Such examples could be multiplied without difficulty. There is no lack of areas to be investigated; what we do lack is concerted action at the level of theological research.

Final Reference to the Magisterium

We have insisted on the usefulness and abiding value of that theological collaboration which can be so fruitful and was so desired by the synod. Our intention was not to submit the magisterium to the authority of theologians, but rather to achieve a fully informed magisterium, conscious of all the aspects of a problem, and thus better enabled to speak the authentic word: a word truly human and truly divine.

It has often been remarked that the council usually restricted itself in its expressions so as not to enter into theological controversy. The conciliar doctrinal commission quite willingly opted for a text which expressed a truth of faith while remaining free of theological opinions still freely discussed. This is a good illustration of the value of theological contribution in order to elucidate doctrinal affirmations and weigh the meaning of each word. At the same time, it illustrates how the magisterium performs its own function in teaching the truth. More than ever, in a world characterized by anarchy in the realm of ideas, there is a necessity for this doctrinal function which the Lord confided to the apostles and in a special way to Peter. It is an inestimable benefit for the Catholic church to have in Peter and his successors a living center of reference and of communion in the faith. Our Lord once said, "I have prayed for you, Simon, that your faith may not fail, and once you have turned back to me, you must strengthen your brothers" (Lk. 22, 31).

It is because Rome is and should remain a focal point that its message must be the measure of catholicity. The church is Latin and Greek, Eastern and Western: the word of God cannot be tied down. This word must be free of any human gloss and pass beyond the schools in order to be "all things to all men." In a world which is becoming more and more unified, the church lives its catholicity at the dimension of continents. Its word must be as pure as a spring and as large as the sea. In proposing theological coresponsibility, we have the conviction of contributing to the most authentic radiance of the church itself.

VII.

The Coresponsibility of Deacons

The Doctrinal Basis of the Diaconate

Pope Pius XII had already opened the way for the restoration of a permanent diaconate in the Latin church by declaring that "the question is not yet sufficiently mature." This was a discreet invitation to continue research. The council considered the problem and resolved it, as we know, by restoring a permanent diaconate for both married and unmarried men. Undoubtedly this decision was made for pastoral reasons, but these were not the only factors operative. The restoration of a permanent diaconate finds its fundamental clarification and justification in the sacramental character of the diaconate itself.

At the council, we attempted to present the doctrinal basis of this return to tradition. Allow us to present here the essentials of that intervention:

152

Those who are opposed to the establishment of a permanent diaconate forget, it seems, that this question concerns the very structure of the church. It is not pragmatic realism which governs this choice of a permanent diaconate, but rather supernatural realism, based on faith and concerned with the sacramental nature of the diaconate. I do not wish to enter here into questions which are still discussed, such as the correct interpretation of the pericope which relates the choice of Stephen and the six other deacons (Acts 6, 1–6).

There are, however, some facts clearly established by a study of the New Testament, the early apostolic fathers (especially Clement of Rome and Ignatius of Antioch), the constant tradition which follows, and the liturgical books of both East and West. In the apostolic and sub-apostolic church, certain charisms of the sacred ministry were attributed in a particular and stable way, to a well-defined level of the priesthood. This level seems to have been established with a view toward providing the bishop with direct aid. It appeared especially in regard to taking care of the poor, the maintenance of good order in the community, the fraternal preparation for the liturgy of the breaking of bread (Acts 2, 42; 4, 32–35; Heb. 13, 16), and the forming of groups of the faithful in the church (as we would say, authentic religious communities).

There are those who do not understand, or seem to understand but poorly, the sacred and liturgical nature of this activity by which a community is formed in order to gather a church. Perhaps their perspective is colored by an imprecise understanding of the nature of the church. The church is founded on the sacraments and thus also on the charisms that derive from the sacrament of orders.

It has been said that the duties proposed for deacons could be confided equally well to laymen, but the question is not one of confiding certain responsibilities (presiding at prayer, catechetical teaching, responsibility for social work) in any way at all to no matter whom. Such responsibilities should only be entrusted to those who, in an objective and adequate way, are endowed with the graces necessary to fulfill them. This guarantees that supernatural efficacy will not be lacking in the development of a true community. Otherwise the church cannot be a truly supernatural society, the true mystical body of Christ, built up in its structure on its ministers and on the graces given to them by God.

The gifts and graces given to the laity in baptism and confirmation do not suffice for the building up of the body of Christ, even when these laymen are deeply animated by an authentic supernatural spirit. Since God has provided other gifts to be used at the service of the community as such, we do not have the right to ignore them, or to refuse to actualize those elements which form a part of the church's patrimony.

According to the divine plan, the bishop receives from God the fullness of the sacred ministry. He receives at the same time the task of building all the supernatural communities that are necessary for his people. That is why the bishop has the capacity to confer upon his "ministers," his "helpers," that kind of share in his powers which is adapted to the needs of his people and to the local and temporal circumstances of his activities.

In the practical order, there are two situations which seem particularly to argue for the necessity of the diaconate. First, when there is question of a very small community obliged to live in the diaspora, cut off from any other group of Christians because of differences in religion, geographical distances or political circumstances. Second, when there is question of vast concentrations of people, especially in and around our cities, who must be aided in rediscovering the intimate and family dimension of the church.

Thus we would base the re-establishment of the diaconate not on the appearance of new needs, but on the need for a sacramental character corresponding to functions recognized as diaconal, and deriving from the very nature of the church's hierarchical structure. Since the council accepted the principle of a diaconate which is considered a permanent rank in the church and not merely a step on the way to the priesthood, Pope Paul VI defined its manner of existing in his motu proprio, *Sacrorum Diaconatus ordinem.*

Before going on to treat of the field of action now open to diaconal coresponsibility, let us first briefly consider the nature of the diaconate itself.

The Specific Place of the Diaconate

THE SACRAMENTAL DIACONATE

At the very outset we should present the permanent diaconate in its true light. We should state that, in restoring the diaconate, we are not trying to supply for the lack of priests. We must avoid at all costs committing once again the error so prevalent at the beginning of the formation of Catholic Action groups. Very often Catholic Action was presented as a means, as "the" means, of making up for the lack of priests. The diaconate is a specific ministry distinct from the priestly ministry. The fact that the number of priests may be equal to fulfilling their role does not at all diminish the duty for lay people to be apostolic, since this duty derives from their baptism. In the same way, the diaconate could not be phased out even if tomorrow the crisis of priestly vocations were resolved. A deacon should not appear to be a "second-class" priest, a means of supplying for a priest. The diaconate should be presented for what it is: a distinct sacramental function.

Canon J. Huard has written,

The diaconate has always pertained to the hierarchical order of the church. From New Testament times, deacons have appeared at the side of bishops and presbyters, and according to both Eastern and Western tradition they receive a solemn ordination by the im-

155

position of hands. They are no longer laymen because they have now been admitted to the first level of the sacrament of orders. Thus it makes no sense to speak of a lay diaconate. Even if the diaconate is conferred upon married men, it loses nothing of its sacramental character, and it effects a definitive consecration of him who receives it, making him a member of the ordained hierarchy.

The diaconate has always pertained to the hierarchical order of episcopacy, not of the presbyterate. *The Apostolic Tradition* of Hippolytus (3rd century) states that the deacon is not ordained to the priesthood, but to the ministry of the bishop.[1]

AN INTEGRATED DIACONATE

The diaconate, then, is a sacramental function distinct from that of the priesthood, and must have a function integrated within the profound unity of the whole of the church's ministry.

There is but one ecclesiastical ministry, one priesthood, possessed in its fullness by the apostolic college, and in relation to this, in a subordinate way, by the members of the presbyterate and the diaconate. Both of these are essentially collaborators with the bishop, and their participation in the ecclesiastical ministry is determined by the church. This participation can vary according to circumstances and situations, and can evolve in the future . . . But it is most important to understand well that close association and essential cooperation which creates a whole, bishops, priests and deacons, who are consecrated under diverse but coordinated forms to the *same ministry. They must represent Christ the Lord, assembling and building up his church* with a view to its eschatalogical fulfillment. The diverse tasks proper to each ministry assume their correlative place and their meaning within this one vast perspective.[2]

1. "Des diacres en Belgique?", in *Revue diocésaine de Tournai*, 22 (1967), p. 34.
2. J. Giblet, *L'Eglise de Vatican II*, Paris, 1966, III, p. 926.

A FULL DIACONATE

It is most important that we place the restored diaconate within the full vision of the ministry opened up to us by Vatican II.

We could summarize the teaching of Vatican II on the ministry by saying that there has been a transition from a narrow concept of cult function to a much wider notion which is also more in keeping with the gospel. In other words the bishops, priests and deacons are not defined first and foremost by their exercise of sacramental cult (though this, of course, is in no way neglected), but rather in terms of their various responsibilities in regard to the evangelization of the world. This implies no opposition, it is rather a development. No one is saying that the sacramental ministry should be considered secondary or arbitrary; rather, this new view gives to the ministry its full extension and takes its point of origin from the preaching of the gospel. In this same line of thinking, we can understand that the diaconal ministry cannot be reduced to this or that sacramental function, but must include all of ecclesial activity from the announcing of the good news to the celebration of the eucharist.

Since it might be possible to conclude from this that the hierarchical ministry is restricted to the interior life of the church that it assembles, we should further note that Vatican II did not only unify once again word and cult, at the heart of the ecclesial community; it also bound together hierarchical pastorate and specifically missionary activity directed toward unbelievers, at the heart of the world. The hierarchical ministry is thus as necessary for the church scattered in the diaspora, as it is for the church assembled to hear the word. This means that every ministry in the church of Christ receives a direct missionary responsibility. Many times the council reminded bishops that their first duty was to announce Christ's salvation to those who do not know it, and many times the same council told priests that their task includes a mission to unbelievers. We are permitted to think that the diaconate is no less free of this

157

responsibility. It would be as false to deny to a deacon the exercise of an authentic mission to unbelievers as it would be to refuse him access to the sanctuary under the pretext that he should live in the world.[3]

Diaconal Coresponsibility

We have thus defined and located the diaconal ministry. Tomorrow's deacon, whether married or not, sees opening up before him a field of action much greater than that known in the early church, but which is faithful to the same inspiration. Deacons will assume functions to be exercised at a parochial level or at less extensive levels—for example, responsibility for a group of families, or for a section of the parish. But there is nothing to prohibit him from exercising these functions at levels more extensive than that of a parish, whether it be a diocese, a nation or even the world. At all of these levels the potentials for his activity are varied: they could be missionary, catechetical, familial, social and so on.

It seems to us that the factor which pleads most strongly for a permanent diaconate to be established soon and over wide areas is the unique possibility that it offers us of giving to our Christian communities a truly human dimension. Priests rightfully complain that they are confronted with parishes that are no longer communities, even when these are not transient parishes, parishes where people do no more than "hang their hat," so to speak. To confide to one or even to many men a care of thousands of souls is to

3. H. Denis and R. Schaller, *Diacres dans le monde d'aujourd'hui. Textes conciliaires et postconciliaires avec commentaire et point de la recherche*, Lyon, 1967, pp. 61–63.

commit the ministry to a task exceeding human capabilities, and to open the door to discouragement. The concentration of population in the cities is a growing fact. One need not have read Harvey Cox's *The Secular City* to be able to see buildings and skyscrapers changing the face of our urban areas.

Decentralization is imperative. It will take the form of a multiplication of places of cult and of meeting. Groups must be more numerous and smaller if they wish to remain human; but this means that there must be more people able to take charge of these groups. It is easy to see in such a situation what the role of the deacons would be: collaborators with the bishops and priests they can restore a family atmosphere, a fraternal warmth to groups suffering from overgrowth. It will require imagination, research and real effort to succeed in creating this kind of pastoral activity of manageable proportions, but the benefits of such an achievement in terms of human communication are inestimable.

What we have just said of the vast city parishes is valid also, though for the opposite reason, in regard to scattered rural parishes. It would be easy to confide to a deacon a good proportion of those tasks which now pertain to the priestly ministry. It is difficult not to be pained when we think of priests isolated, living far away from one another, and suffering from the fact that they do not have a ministry equal to their capacities or their zeal. And it is easy to envisage these priests as leaders of a team, animating from one center, groups of the faithful directed locally by their deacons.

The success of the apostolate is linked to its capacity to assume a truly human dimension. The anonymous mass in which the believer finds himself lost can hardly appear to him as a church, as the family of God assembled around the eucharist, as a home which he leaves to go out to the world and to which he returns in order to be once again with his brothers. One of the reasons for the attraction which small sects exercise over their members (we are thinking here especially of Latin America), lies precisely in their nature as sects, small groups, where everybody knows everybody else. They are personal societies where each one feels himself a real member of a spiritual family. Can we not say that this paradoxical example proves with urgency how necessary it is for us to reduce our ecclesial communities to a size which is human?

In this line of thought, the institution of permanent local deacons, leaders of small groups, offers a lot of hope for the future. They would exercise a pastoral mission of a degree and type dictated by the concrete situation in which they find themselves. A whole world of new experiences is available to them.

But let us not limit our desire to see groups of a human size only in regard to geographical parishes. There are many other aspects of church which can be given life by the same desire. There is talk today of sociological parishes, groups of Christians bound together by a common interest or occupation: universities, industry, medicine, the professions and so forth. Here too, smaller groups, created with the help of deacons, would result in more intimate contact.

There is no domain which would be so suited to a married deacon as that area, hardly investigated, of the apostolate to the family. Priests can help couples prepare for marriage, to live it out and discover its riches. The married deacon can bring the contribution of his own experience to groups engaged in family activity. Whether the deacon himself be a doctor, lawyer or social worker, the wealth of his contribution would be immense.

Then too, the experience and professional competency of deacons placed at the service of the Christian community can aid this community in setting up structures and organizations, and in keeping them supple. Those deacons who were free of the responsibilities of civil life could easily exercise a part of their coresponsibility in ecclesial life even at a high level. They have a full right to a place in the diocesan pastoral council, as well as in the parish council. Because their commitment is enduring, their activity will have a continuity, thus supplying for a frequent defect in many enterprises undertaken with good will but always forced to lead a precarious existence.

The Call of the Church

The horizon opens up and extends beyond view: "The harvest is great." May we not be obliged to add, "but the workers are few"? Through the voice of Vatican II the Lord is calling many laymen to answer this new vocation.

He addresses his call to every level of society: workers, manual or intellectual, doctors, lawyers, engineers and businessmen. He calls them as they are: in their work clothes, with their capacities and their limitations. The tasks which the church wishes to confide to them are many and varied. It foresees a training for them which is supple and tailored to their needs, governed by the consideration of definite tasks to be accomplished. We must develop a new pedagogy, and for this the cooperation of the future candidates themselves is necessary. The church enters, as does

161

the man in the gospel, into the hiring place, and finds many workers there because no one had hired them. It asks them to understand the spiritual distress of the world, and to share their bread, that is, their Christianity, with those who hunger sometimes not knowing why. The church invites these men to draw from their faith the courage to make decisions that will not be easy because they involve renunciation and sacrifice. For, normally, these married deacons will earn their livelihood and continue to exercise their profession, harmonizing their various duties with their functions as deacons. This twofold demand may well mean renunciation on the material level. There will be time invested in just being available, there will be responsibilities to share with others, and there will be hours given over to the service of the Lord which could have been dedicated to business or recreation. The Lord is inviting them to hear a call to evangelical poverty and to give themselves. Each one must respond to this call personally, in a way which is both balanced and generous.

A married deacon cannot answer such a call before having consulted his family. He must weigh the pros and cons of the situation with the realism of faith and with realism in general, taking into account the thoughts of his wife and children. The wife of a deacon must understand the duty and importance of the call made to him with whom she shares her life. Her consent is essential at the very beginning of her husband's vocation and her commitment will be necessary to him if he is to live it out. Her sustaining and encouraging role is vital to her husband because outside his family he will have to face a good deal of misunderstanding and perhaps even mockery. He will easily find many people to reproach him for sacrificing his family

162

and involving himself in things which, after all, belong to priests. He will have to go on in the night. No one can guarantee him either the understanding of lay people or the warm understanding of all the priests whose close collaborator he will be. For these too must find their place again in a whole new complex of unexplored situations, not all of which will be comfortable. He will have to walk on the water with his eyes fixed on the Lord, buoyed up by generosity and consistency. He will overcome the contrary winds, provided that he does not concentrate on the waves under his feet, but upon the face of the Lord inviting him to follow.

To insure success, the first men to experiment should be those who have already succeeded in their profession, in their family life, or, to put it briefly, in the business of being a man. For these first deacons will be closely watched by people ready to criticize. The first soldiers out of the trench, those who open the breach, have, when the mission is a success, a glorious role, but one which takes more than common courage. These first volunteers will have to create the image of the diaconate. The generation to follow will have an easier time of it. "One sows and another reaps," the Lord says. The church is looking for pioneers.

But a delicate problem arises here: will not vocations to the diaconate further reduce vocations to the priesthood? We do not think so. The church is open to diversity. There are vocations to the diocesan priesthood and to the religious life, and within this latter there is a multiple variety of orders and congregations all existing side by side. Furthermore, the ultimate reason for introducing permanent deacons is precisely to create and multiply centers where the Christian life is lived more intensely. These vital and

163

generous communities should, in the nature of things, give rise to priestly and religious vocations, to contemplatives and missionaries. Let us have confidence that the Holy Spirit will know how to harmonize the charisms of each one for the over-all good of the church.

From now on educators and others who exercise influence in the church—journalists, writers, lecturers—should aid in making known this new form of coresponsibility. They should help to create that atmosphere of sympathy and receptivity absolutely indispensable for the success of this experiment.

The future will tell what forms and expressions of the permanent diaconate will characterize the 20th and 21st centuries. At the same time, we must look to the past and be inspired by the radiance reflected on the face of a St. Stephen, "a man full of faith and of the Holy Spirit." Yet the Spirit is still at work, still creating. It is with reason that people speak of a diaconate as a hopeful sign on the horizon. We need a minimum of juridicism and a maximum of docility to the Holy Spirit and of suppleness as we exercise this coresponsibility which is at once traditional and new, rooted in the past and stretching out to the future.

VIII.

The Coresponsibility of Religious

The council dedicated a decree to the appropriate renewal of the religious life. The text as we have it is a sort of compromise between two theologies which confronted one another at the council. Though the document sketches out some measures to be taken for the adaptation necessary today, it stopped half way, despite the 14,000 amendments made to it before the voting. The two theological tendencies could not but cancel one another out since each was represented by about half of the votes.

But if the decree is itself somewhat lacklustre, the renewal of the religious life has received valuable directives and inspiration from the major documents of the council. We are thinking in particular of the *Constitution on the Church,* and the *Constitution on the Church in the Modern World,* as well as other texts, such as the *Declaration on Religious Freedom.*

There emerges from these texts a fresh vision of the mystery of the church: the people of God on the march, a community at once missionary and committed to the service of the world.

This deeper penetration in understanding the church as a whole implies an obligation to reconsider that authentic and privileged expression of the church—as a part within the whole—which is the religious life properly so called. The renewal of this life reflects the renewal of the Christian life itself. The religious life cannot be considered in isolation, as though it were something outside of or on the periphery of the church's life. It is rather an intensely and eminently Christian existence, bearing within itself, to the highest degree, the fundamental and universal demands of baptism.

To be a true religious one must be a Christian living out all the consequences of baptism and a person fully able to assume his own responsibilities. To be a religious woman means to be a woman completely fulfilling her role in the church and the world of today. The implications of these demands entail a renewal in depth which cannot but be a source of joy as it becomes manifest.

The Religious as a Christian

If there is one message to be derived from the council, it is the importance of baptism as the basis of all Christian life and of all consecration to God. Baptismal consecration is already a total thing. One eucharistic host is neither more nor less consecrated than another; it either is, or is not, consecrated. There are diverse functions in the church yet there is but one baptism, just as there is for all Christians but one call to perfection, and one vocation to holiness. The

166

council itself, in order to avoid any confusion in this matter, refrained from using the ancient but ambiguous phrase "the states of perfection."

Religious life does not change the fundamental implications of baptism. If the whole church must be missionary and present to the world, it follows that each baptized person must incarnate the demands of this mission and this presence in his own life situation and in keeping with his own vocation.

The religious vocation itself must obey this law and by that very fact is at the service of all. It grows out of baptism as a flower grows from its bud so that, in its turn, it can aid all the baptized to become more aware of their own reality. This is what the council has to say:

> The profession of the evangelical counsels, then, appears as a sign which can and ought to attract all the members of the church to an effective and prompt fulfillment of the duties of their Christian vocation. The people of God has no lasting city here below, but looks forward to one which is to come. This being so, the religious state by giving its members greater freedom from earthly cares more adequately manifests to all believers the presence of heavenly goods already possessed here below.
>
> Furthermore, it not only witnesses to the fact of a new and eternal life acquired by the redemption of Christ. It foretells the resurrected state and the glory of the heavenly kingdom. Christ also proposed to his disciples that form of life which he, as the Son of God, accepted in entering this world to do the will of the Father. In the church this same state of life is imitated with particular accuracy and perpetually exemplified. The religious state reveals in a unique way that the kingdom of God and its overmastering necessities are superior to all earthly considerations. Finally, to all men it shows wonderfully at work within the church the surpassing greatness of the force of Christ the King and the boundless power of the Holy Spirit.

167

Thus, although the religious state constituted by the profession of the evangelical counsels does not belong to the hierarchical structure of the Church, nevertheless it belongs inseparably to its life and holiness (*Constitution on the Church,* art. 44).

OBEDIENCE

Baptism's inner dynamism present within the depths of the religious life reveals its demands not only within the church as a whole, but also in the practice of the religious life itself, especially in regard to the concept and exercise of obedience which plays such a large role in the religious life.

Often in inculcating the virtue of obedience, insufficient attention has been devoted to the fact that this obedience is a Christian reality and not simply a moral virtue. A certain kind of obedience at one time too prevalent was insufficiently integrated into the mystery of Christ living in us through baptism: it tended to accentuate its ascetic aspect to the detriment of its own mystical fullness.

This obedience, more deist than Christian, was partly influenced by those social and political structures deriving from the notion of the "divine right" of kings, and found expression in a whole world of spiritual literature. Today, for those who are sensitive to the movements inspired by the council, it seems to be almost a caricature of the true meaning of obedience. But as a matter of fact, such a view has not wholly disappeared.

The Older View of Obedience. In the older view, obedience was presented primarily as an exercise of virtue: forgetfulness of self, renunciation, mortification. Obedience

168

led one to abandon one's own judgment and personal will into the hands of the superior. Not only did one await orders, one ought to foresee the slightest wishes of authority; even if authority can be wrong, one is never wrong in obeying.

A close similarity between a religious community and a family was preached as the ideal to attain. And thus phrases like "mother" or "daughter" were used, certain attitudes and gestures were prescribed, and custom books saw to the least detail of comportment. Obedience was based on an abstract rule applied in common, rather than on the persons themselves and their differences. It was directed rather toward the carrying out of a given order than toward collaboration in accomplishing a goal. Dialogue with authority never entered in as a factor to be desired, constitutive of the obedience relationship itself.

If, happily, there are many reactions against this type of obedience, it still remains more widespread than one would generally believe, even if, in regard to this or that point, the actual situation does not meet (or exceed) the description presented here. We are dealing with a tendency profoundly rooted in the traditions of recent centuries and which will not disappear overnight. We cannot presume that just because certain outdated practices have been abolished, a renewed concept of obedience already animates the community as a whole.

Obedience as Communion with Christ. The renewal of the theology of obedience has opened up perspectives which once again give to Christ his central place at the very heart of obedience.

169

The primary truth which has thus been re-established in the forefront of any consideration of obedience and which should be a predominant attitude of soul is this: he who obeys enters in to the very obedience of Christ himself. "I no longer live, it is Christ who lives in me" (Gal. 2, 20), that is to say, it is no longer that religious who obeys, it is Christ in him who obeys the will of the Father, for the salvation of the world.

Thus, obedience shares in the mystery of Christ himself. It stands forth not only as an obedience to God or to Christ present in the superior, but as the obedience of Christ himself being accomplished in us. In obeying, we enter into the mystery of the Son's filial dependence upon his Father, that Son who humbled himself and became "obedient to death, even to death on the cross."

Obedience finds its true greatness only when it is rooted in such depths. Christ obeyed his Father *for the salvation of the world*. It is at the service of the redemption: it is essentially missionary in all the manifold meaning of the word. Obedience is inwardly directed toward the service of a church which is in a state of being missionary: in virtue of its own secret dynamism it obeys this inner movement of the church. All, "superiors" as well as "inferiors," share in this filial obedience of Christ to his Father. The "superior" far from being contrasted with his "subordinates" as he who commands to those who must obey, rather presents himself to them as he who obeys first, totally committed to the will of the Father and who brings the others in his train. He is the servant of the ideal, of the common good, of the best which each member has within himself. The superior is the first to walk this way of obedience to God, to Christ, to the gospel and to the church.

170

Pope Paul VI beautifully expressed the nature of obedience "in Christ" when he said in an allocution:

We believe that both the spirit and the forms of obedience have received a regeneration from the council. It would take a long time to explain. But if we have understood anything of the central doctrine of the council on the mystery of the church, we will be easily convinced that obedience is something more than a purely formal and juridical homage to ecclesiastical laws and submission to ecclesiastical authority. It is a penetration and acceptance of the mystery of Christ, who has saved us by means of obedience. It is a continuation and an imitation of his fundamental act: his "yes" to the will of his Father. It is an understanding of the principle which dominates the whole plan of the incarnation and the redemption (see *Constitution on the Church*, art. 3).

And so you see, obedience becomes an assimilation to Christ, the divine obedient One. It becomes the fundamental norm of our pedagogy of Christian formation. It becomes the indispensable index of the inner unity of the church, the source and the sign of its peace. It becomes a fruitful cooperation in the church's mission of spreading the good news. It becomes an ascetical exercise of humility and a spiritual exercise of charity (see Phil. 2, 5–12). It becomes communion with Christ and with the person who, by Christ, is his apostle and representative for us.[1]

Obedience as Communion with the Church. An obedience which is thus lived and inserted in the obedience of Christ to his Father must of necessity live in the church. Christ is inseparable from his body; Christian obedience cannot but be an ecclesial obedience.

Obedience discovers its own dimensions first and foremost within the church, and therefore it is right to insist strongly upon this primacy of the church, the ecclesial

1. Address to General Audience, October 5, 1966.

community. Since it affects the very life of all the particular communities within it, the church can, in virtue of its priority, impose upon them the characteristics of its own life. That is why the council ordered each religious congregation to enter into the biblical, liturgical and apostolic renewal present in the church of our day, and in this light to revise their constitutions and directories. Not only must each member, individually, be "of the church," but the community as such sharing in the obedience of Christ must do the same in, by and through the church.

Normally, when we speak of church, we mean the particular church which is present to the religious community and requires that each community find its place, according to its own charism, integrating itself within the pastoral efforts of the whole, under the leadership of its head. There is no question here of renouncing the apostolic goals specific to each religious community, but rather of having these communities open themselves to coresponsibility in union with all. There are diocesan pastoral councils coming into being in response to the appeal of the council. These are asking religious, along with priests, deacons and the laity, to assume their full role in the pastoral work of the church so that awareness of our active and concrete solidarity may become part of the daily life of the church of tomorrow.

The Religious as a Responsible Person

The council accentuated not only the value of baptism, but also the value of personalism and its implications. The rights of the human person along with the correlative

172

responsibilities they entail are inalienable and sacred, and they must be recognized within the very heart of religious communities. When well understood, these rights and responsibilities, far from being a "source of trouble," are valuable factors for renewal. Respect for these rights is in no way opposed to the true practice of obedience; but rather, just the contrary.

Is it necessary to recall that one who obeys neither amputates nor annihilates his personality in order to serve the common good? The community has need of the contribution of each one with all his riches and potential. Opposed to the good of others and of the whole is not personality, but the refusal of the gift of self. One can never be too personal. The only danger lies in being not personal enough by enclosing oneself in individualism.

To obey is to become more personal, in the sense that one discovers with ever greater freedom and clarity that a person does not exist or fulfill himself except by establishing authentic bonds with others and by becoming part of a community or communities. Obedience is not primarily a response to a command or to a discipline. It is born of a fundamental need of the human person who can only be fulfilled in finding his true place in relation to others.

To obey is to direct one's own will, rectifying it insofar as it is individualistic, shortsighted and self-involved. This does not limit the personality, but rather allows it to develop fully and acquire its true dimensions as a being rooted in the human, a being of relations.

The council fully recognized these demands of personalism when it stated that "all the faithful, clerical and lay, possess a lawful freedom of inquiry and of thought and the freedom to express their minds humbly and courageously

173

about those matters in which they enjoy competence" (*Modern World,* art. 62). All of this must be accepted and lived out in the daily life of religious communities.

If relationships are to be real, then the obedience of an adult must be an adult obedience. Passivity and conformism are not synonyms for obedience. All that smacks of maternalism or paternalism on the one hand, or its echo, childishness, on the other, must be pitilessly cut out. Thus the way will lie open for the coresponsibility so necessary within religious communities. For these, as we have said, stand in need of the contribution of each one, the common sharing of each individual charism for the common good of the whole.

At one time, the constitutions of religious orders forbade or strictly limited the relationships between the religious themselves, centering the community around the superior as far as possible. This derived from a conception of monarchy after the manner of the *ancien régime* as well as from the "moralistic" spirituality described above.

At the moment, people are rediscovering the degree to which it is necessary to live "in community," that is, not only in indispensable union with authority, but also in a true communion with one another. This supposes that there be true mutual exchange, a common sharing of one's activities and more profoundly still a sharing of what one is, or what one wishes to be, in the service of the Lord.

Obedience lived out in coresponsibility is a dynamic force for progress. Too often obedience has wrongly appeared as a brake on personal initiative. What inspirations and energies have been lost because of a vow of obedience badly understood or badly lived! Authentic obedience is not the servant of immobility or the status quo, or of the rule

174

considered as an aim in itself. It is, rather, at the service of life and of a search undertaken in common. No doubt, obedience sometimes acts as a brake, but this is necessary in any vehicle. A brake is not designed to render a vehicle immobile in one place, but rather to allow it to go more quickly, since we know that it is always there and can be used whenever necessary. Such an obedience is expansive. "I have run the way of your commandments because you have opened up my heart," the psalmist says.

Thus what we are discussing is the furthering of communities of persons. This means that the person be recognized as an end in himself, according to the variety of his gifts and in keeping with his own rhythm of growth; and it implies that, if the community is at the service of its persons, these, for their part, must recognize the community itself as an expression of that common good which authority is trying to foster.

Respect for personalism requires a revision of the once-classic formation given in the novitiate. In the perspective of an "extrinsic" obedience as described above, efforts were made to mold each candidate according to a uniform cast; each one must pass through the same steps during the same amount of time within a life situation completely cut off from the world and deprived of any apostolic activity.

It is hoped that the new canon law which is being written will free itself from the narrowness of the past, and that a new vision will dominate the stages and conditions of formation. It must be a formation which takes account of the fact that today's novices often possesses a maturity and experience of life greater than heretofore, and also of the fact that from now on, in all areas, a continual formation should be foreseen, a formation which develops in a cycle

175

and lasts throughout all of life. Vocations will depend in large measure upon the way in which pedagogical principles, suited for the furtherance of an authentic personalism in the world of today, are respected.

THE WOMAN RELIGIOUS AS A WOMAN

We have said that a religious must be a Christian and a fully developed person. We now wish to speak about women religious.

It must be admitted simply: the ecclesiastical world has not yet recognized and accepted that increased role of woman which is today an accomplished and uncontested fact, at least in the developed countries. John XXIII made reference to this fact in *Pacem in Terris,* and the Third World Congress of the Lay Apostolate held in Rome in October 1967 gave it expression in a very significant resolution:

The Third World Congress of the Lay Apostolate formulates the desire to see granted to woman all the rights and all the responsibilities of the Christian within the Catholic church, and that a serious doctrinal study be undertaken on the place of woman in the sacramental order and in the Church.

The congress asks moreover:

(1) that competent women be made part of all pontifical commissions,

(2) that qualified women be consulted with regard to the revision of the canon law, especially those that concern women,

in order that feminine dignity be fully recognized and that the greatest possibilities in the service of the Church be granted to woman.

The role of woman is not yet fully recognized; it is a

goal yet to be achieved. We can see a good indication of this situation if we but think back to the tremors produced by the idea of inviting women as lay auditors to the council and to the resistance which had to be overcome—by the highest recourse—in order to allow women to receive communion along with the men at the mass celebrated in the conciliar aula. So long as the men in the church, taken as a whole, are not aware of the numerous anomalies which have yet to be overcome, the renewal of the religious life of women will be paralyzed. Let us be realists: the men in the church will never discover these anomalies by themselves; it is up to the women religious to point them out and secure the necessary corrections.

It is not a question of having women step out of their own role, but simply of the emancipation due to women religious in our time. These religious have the duty and the right to assume their responsibilities, not only in those questions which concern them as women, but also in all the vital problems of humanity. The woman religious, as a woman, has a contribution to make to the church and to the world.

Recently a superior who is particularly qualified and representative wrote to us personally as follows:

Isn't it true that wherever a woman religious has been received without suspicion, with interest and respect, she has introduced a quality of freshness and spontaneity into relationships?

The church is often accused of writing a great deal and doing too little. Would a greater share in feminine intuition do any harm to theologians? Would not the influence of women result in a more rapid transition from thought to action?

And as for women religious themselves, would not contact with more complex situations serve as a factor to make them more open,

177

to help them go beyond the limits of their own activity and the outlook of their own congregation?

Then, after underlining the great necessity for preparing religious for these new tasks, she goes on:

How often do religious experience a situation in which they are really "partners"?

Most often when they are invited to a meeting designed for research into some subject or other, are they not invited in restricted numbers or as "auditors"? Or again, when they are assembled in greater or less number, how often are they placed in a subordinate position in regard to some ecclesiastic who "presides"?

If they were invited to collaborate fully in an atmosphere of truth and simplicity, then they could be themselves, that is, they could be fully "present," and perhaps effective.

There is no question here of a stormy victory for overt feminism nor of triumphalism. But why doubt that the religious would be completely in her place within the church of today, which wishes to be a "poor and serving" church?

In this same line of thought, women religious can bring new factors into play—often very feminine ones—toward the solution of problems which up to this time have always been approached without her. "One only sees well with the heart." Without wishing to reserve exclusively for woman this way of looking at things, it is still certain that she has "her own" way of approaching problems.

John XXIII, Paul VI, Athenagoras and others, have they not done more for ecumenism by their gentleness and understanding, than all the research and laborious discussion of the theologians?

Cannot women religious contribute a more direct collaboration with those who are studying the great problems of our world: hunger, development, peace? Someone will object, and with reason, that religious are already overburdened. It is not a matter of having

178

them do more, but of considering them another way. They are not "employees," they are "partners."

These words invite reflection. In order to do justice to their legitimate requests one must make large use of the "principle of subsidiarity" to which the council made reference more than once. According to this principle, each authority should be recognized as competent in its own proper sphere, and recourse should be had to higher authority only in cases of real need. This principle should be applied as well in the structuring of religious life.

As a result of the council, a step was made toward decentralization by the erection of a consultative world commission of women religious which is to meet each year in Rome. Another step was taken by the nomination of four nuns and an undersecretary to the Congregation of Religious; they are responsible for certain problems specific to women religious. We are approaching, then, a full recognition of the equality of men and women religious in the church. But this in no way implies, if this need be said at all, that there is an identity of role and function. Right now, the code of canon law is being rewritten. Now is the opportune time to free the religious life from some of the impediments of the past and, with the active cooperation of the women religious themselves, to open out the religious life to the great summons of our time.

Tracing the Course of Development

We are at a crossroads. There is a disturbing decline in religious vocations, and at the same time there are many leaving the classical forms of religious life for the sake of a style of apostolic life which is more supple. There are many reasons for this twofold phenomenon. But it should never happen that one of these reasons be our slowness to begin necessary renewal.

While they await the revision of canon law and the creation of certain means of renewal, it is the duty of those who are responsible in our religious communities to draw attention to necessary adaptations and to contribute actively to the search for solutions. And this is but the beginning of the contribution one has the right to expect from them.

For the moment, a considerable step will have been taken if all the possibilities for adaptation opened up by the *Decree on the Appropriate Renewal of the Religious Life,* incomplete as it may be, are resolutely followed up. Wherever there is a tendency toward immobility we still find inertia and a static situation. The sight of anachronistic religious habits still unchanged or imperceptibly modified, which one can see at any international congress, suffices in itself to show that the break between the church and the world of the 20th century still exists in this area and that this counter-witness is still with us.

Some real progress can be noted in regard to renewal and it seems to be growing. Here and there it is impeded by some extravagant abuse in regard to modernization which the international press sets out for all to see, and which furnishes those who have opted for the status quo, an easy excuse and an easy conscience.

If the renewal desired by the council is ever to attain the dimensions desired for it, then there must be a more vivid awareness within the religious communities themselves of their proper coresponsibility. Much could be done if those congregations which are more advanced in adaptation, were to offer their help to other congregations which have but begun to adapt. In this regard, the associations of major superiors could make a group contribution by organizing congresses, workshops and meetings where experiences could be shared and directions more clearly defined. The pilot congregations should be invited to take some positions of responsibility: this need not mean that they are meddling, but rather that they are offering their collaboration and fraternal support. There are large gaps between institutions, at a national or worldwide level, and sometimes within the same congregation whose extension is worldwide these same gaps appear. What a great benefit it would be for those congregations who have but begun to open out toward adaptation, if they were able to rely on other congregations who have succeeded in the renewal, with the confidence that they would not thereby lose their own autonomy.

If exchanging and sharing serve to stimulate all, they are particularly helpful, it seems to us, for those contemplative communities which often complain of being isolated and of finding difficulties in realizing their renewal. Many superiors of these communities, regardless of what order they belong to, wish to meet with one another, freely discuss their problems, take initiatives at a local level and make their voice heard in the national or Roman meetings. They are also aware of the need, at certain levels, for discussions with communities engaged in the active apostolate. Such contacts, which are mutually enriching, ought to be multiplied in the years to come.

And speaking of contemplative communities, why not desire that their role and their influence extend within the people of God? The disciples once said to Jesus, "Master, teach us to pray." The world has need again today of spiritual masters, of contemplatives, who witness before their brothers of their experience of God and who repeat these words of St. John: "That which we have heard and we have seen with our own eyes; that which we have watched and touched with our hands: the Word who is life —this we announce to you." Christians—and others—have need of places of prayer and silence where they can be renewed, and discover the ultimate meaning of life. Would it not be possible, in a way compatible with their rule— which will eventually be made more supple—for our enclosed religious to make God known to those about them? Could they not open "schools" of faith and spirituality there in their own convents, where they could share with others the riches of their life? St. Catherine of Siena or St. Teresa of Avila, mystics dedicated to the highest contemplation, were at the same time at the heart of the problems in the world of their time. Their lives are a symbol and an invitation. Pius XII already addressed to contemplative nuns a message regarding some type of adapted apostolic activity.

Our contemplatives should read with attention the memorable discourse which Pope Paul VI addressed to the Carmelites. It cannot be adopted completely, perhaps, by contemplative nuns but it does indicate a way of thinking:

You must be willing, as was St. Teresa, to be so aware of the needs of the church and the sufferings of society that they become for you not motives for flight from the world, but of spiritual concern. You must understand your dedication to the love of God as an exercise in the love of your neighbor. You know the urgency and the multiplicity of the church's needs: they so press at the doors of your monasteries and of your cells as to convince you that, in order not to be distracted and interiorly reproached in the

182

exercise of your prayer, you must become missionary monks; and from being solitary contemplatives you must become masters in the Spirit and preachers to your brothers who lack the bread of the gospel, and who are hungry for your spiritual food. From being good Carmelites who know nothing of the pastoral life, you must become excellent pastors, and if it should happen worthy bishops, as has already happened for the honor of your order, the building up of the church of God and the glory of our Lord. We know that this is not your vocation but it can become so when the authority and the charity of the church ask it of you. This gift of yours will in no way impoverish your prayer, but rather plunge it into the fire of experience, of ardor and of love. Whatever you give through this love, you will receive back through the life, the realism and the renewal of your own contemplation.[2]

Every religious, whether contemplative or not, is a privileged person called and chosen by God in view of the salvation of the world. His vocation, far from isolating him from others, concerns them and brings them close to him. If a religious is the beneficiary of an abundance of spiritual life, this is ultimately for the world which hungers and thirsts for God even when it is not aware of its own distress. Let each religious compare what he receives spiritually with what he gives in the same order. How many other Christians are fed each day by the eucharist and the word of God? How many Christians know the grace of regular retreats, of conferences and spiritual talks, of a way of life which fosters union with God? We would dare to say that the religious receives all this "to trade with." He could be accused of being a "spiritual capitalist" if he did not share with the people of God and with the world the goods he has received for their sake.

This is true for all religious without distinction. Someone

2. Allocution to the Carmelites, June 22, 1967.

is rich when compared with anyone who is less rich, and there is no avoiding the duty to share. Amid all the variety of our religious institutions there must be ways of handing on this life; and thus each religious community is summoned to an examination of conscience and a rethinking of its common life inspired by the gospel.

It is too easily said that every consecrated life is apostolic by definition, and that whatever activity is engaged in is apostolic because of the intention which animates it. Even supposing that this is so, it still remains true that human activities, whether they be nursing, teaching or anything else, do not all possess the same apostolic quality, concentration or urgency. It is still true that the christianization of the world, which is confided to all in coresponsibility, is not furthered in the same way by any action whatsoever: there is a hierarchy of values.

We must delineate and actualize those possibilities for a spiritual apostolate which are imminent within the interior of each specific vocation. These possibilities must receive a priority of time, and those things which are less essential must, when there is need, be made less of.

When a field of action is open to coresponsibility over and above the proper sphere of each institute, whether it be a question of the religious domain or that of catechetics, the family, society, is there anyone who cannot then see the value of collaboration among religious? Today Christians in general are vividly aware of a need for spiritual formation and of periodic religious renewal. Many of them desire meetings, weekends and retreats for spiritual revivification. Along with priests and lay people, each one according to his own charism, religious are called more and more to play an active role in this regard as well as in the christianization of family and social life under its many aspects. The doctrinal expression of Christian teaching found in the encyclicals and council documents must be translated into everyday reality and be made available to everyone. How much religious could do, especially those who have in their hands the formation of the wealthy, to initiate these people in the social demands of the gospel and guide them in making a response. Or again, think of all that religious can do within the people of God as a whole to make the spirit of Christianity penetrate in that vast fallow field of the communication media, in the world of leisure, and in that marginal world to be found in all our great cities—that new kind of youth of our day. There are spiritual sufferings and human sufferings voicelessly calling for the mobilization of all available compassion. These are summoning religious to rethink their rule and their way of life in terms of the gospel, in keeping with existing needs, and in close and active communion with all Christians and all men of good will.

The aggiornamento begun by the council has no sense if it does not bring forth an adaptation of rules and customs in the light of our apostolic action which is richer, more daring and more in the spirit of the gospel. In our book *The Nun in the World* we warned against a modernization which would be merely humanistic. We said, "The adaptations we have spoken of do not imply any relaxation or any compromise with the spirit of the world. . . . to adapt apostolically is not to introduce luxury or excessive comfort, nor to follow every craze in order to be right up to the minute, and thus exude an atmosphere of worldliness and superficiality."

The adaptation of the religious life is completely domi-

185

nated by the need to evangelize and humanize the world. We must be free of certain impediments which come from the past, but only so that we can better respond to the call of God today. David set aside Saul's heavy armor so that he could be free to undertake God's combat against Goliath with the aid only of a sling.

The same is true for the conciliar aggiornamento. It will be realized to the degree that it creates suppleness, availability and new life, at the service of the Lord and at the service of men.

IX.

The Coresponsibility of Laymen

The Council and the Laity

History will render glory to the council for having beautifully defined the nature of the church, the people of God, and for having boldly sketched the place and role of the laity in the church. History will no doubt also accuse us of not having sufficiently put into practice that which is so well defined—the coresponsibility of the laity.

Admittedly, during the course of the consultations which preceded the council, some lay experts exercised, within certain commissions, an influence which was not negligible. Then too, during the different sessions, some laymen and later on some laywomen were admitted as auditors, these latter not without some difficulty. Nevertheless, we must admit that neither before the council nor during its progress was there, between the fathers of the council and the lay people, a true dialogue.

It is not that lay people should form a sort of pressure

group and act as though it were a session of congress. Neither is there question of establishing them as judges in matters of faith; this is a role reserved to the magisterium. Nevertheless, they should have been invited to assume real complementary functions.

The formula which describes the deliberation of the Council of Jerusalem, the first in the church's history, contains some lessons for us: "the apostles, the presbyters, and the whole church decided . . ." (Acts 15, 22). The implication is obvious: it was the whole people of God who were engaged in making the decision.

Vatican II met at a time when the theology of the laity was still largely a thing of the future, and it suffered from this lack. The extreme reticence of canon law in its section on the laity is well known. Though the code has some things to say about lay people, the faithful and associations of the faithful, the sum total of what it says is rather meager, and no complete image of the layman emerges from the text.

Since 1917, the year when the code was published, there has been some real progress, but there are many stages yet to be achieved before the life of the layman in the church receives adequate juridical expression.

As is usually the case, life is ahead of law. Since the council, we witness daily the greater part played by the Christian community in the liturgy, we see to what degree pastoral renewal accents and animates the community dimension of the sacraments. Institutions have arisen which actualize the coresponsibility of lay people: there is the parish council, and at the diocesan level the pastoral council, which was established by Vatican II itself.

188

IS THE CHURCH A DEMOCRACY?

The renewal of community in the church, which ultimately derives from faith, naturally finds its place within the progress of a world moving more and more in the direction of democracy. It could seem that as we accentuate the role of the laity we deny the hierarchical character of the church. But this is not true, provided that we understand how the church accepts democracy within herself, and the historical context in which, not authority itself, but its way of being exercised has come about.

The incarnation of the Word took place at a given point in space and time. Christ's personality bears the mark of his place and time of birth. The church carries the same marks; as a human society it bears the imprints of the time in which it lives.

History shows us how, through the course of ages, the concrete way of exercising authority in the church at all its levels has developed. There is an undeniable process of osmosis and imitation between the manner of ruling in the secular world and in the church, and this is to be expected. The church has seen rule of the type of Constantine, feudal lords and enlightened despots. Today most developed countries have adopted a democratic form of government. All of this pertains to the realm of contingency.

It is precisely in this realm that we find a real uneasiness in the church. There is a crisis in confidence, not in authority as such, but in the government of the church as a human system and structure. We meet in books and magazines criticism of the ecclesiastical regime as such independent of any particular personalities. These criticisms are special in that they often come from priests and

189

lay people, devoted children of the church, whose fidelity cannot be doubted, and who suffer from the situation which they deplore. The directing bodies, they say, have a way of functioning which is no longer conformed to the atmosphere of our time, as expressed by the spirit and customs with which we are all familiar in the civil life of democratic regimes. Expressed in this way, such criticism is ambiguous and requires greater clarification.

But let us say right away: our temporal categories are never adequate to express, much less to enclose, the profound mystery of the church. To wish to catalogue the church under the label of monarchy, oligarchy or democracy is a futile task. The church's reality is too rich and too complex to fit within human categories and analogies.

There are within the church elements which are monarchical, others which are oligarchical, and still others which are democratic. The papacy, the bishops, and the laity could be invoked as illustrative of these elements. Within the church there is at one and the same time one principle of unity (monarchy), a pluralism of hierarchical responsibilities (oligarchy), and a fundamental equality of all in the communion of the people of God (democracy). All of these must mutually integrate one another since they are all essential to the truth of the church. The church can admit of no exclusive reliance on any one facet, whether it be papism, episcopalism or conciliarism. The papal primacy has aspects about it which are monarchical, but the papacy is unintelligible except as integrated within a universal episcopate, and in living connection with the whole body. The episcopacy for its part is not a self-sufficient oligarchy, but reaches out in both directions in a twofold living relationship: one, with its leader the pope, and the other with the whole presbyterate and laity.

190

The vocabulary of a given time must be constantly corrected so that it does not prove false to the reality for which it stands. Having made this reservation, we can now say that the Second Vatican Council certainly was characterized by a move in the direction of "democratization" because of the accent it placed on the people of God, by the stress it laid on the hierarchy as a service, and by its creation of certain organisms within the church which favor democratic methods of government.

History teaches us that, while the structure of the church is hierarchical by the very will of its founder, the ways of exercising authority in the church have varied throughout the centuries. It is possible to trace a long history of these variations occasioned by a thousand temporal and contingent factors, whether it be a matter of an election of a pope, the appointment of bishops or practically anything else. All of this was expressed from age to age according to the conditions in which the church found itself. It is normal, then, that our age, characterized by democracy, would also tend, and rightfully so, to influence the human and variable factors of the church, rendering them more apt in governing men of today.

We cannot apply the same norms, as is obvious, to doctrines which pertain to the faith: a credo is not established by a majority vote. The divinity of Jesus Christ, his resurrection from the dead and his presence in the eucharist are not things decided by ballot. The Lord confided to the apostles the mission of expressing and passing on the content of faith, and it is to their successors, the bishops united with Peter and under his authority, that the Lord has assigned the continuance of this task, and has promised the special assistance of the Holy Spirit. The

191

problem, then, is not to know what men desire to hear today, but rather what the Lord wishes to reveal to them.

Every bishop accomplishes his mission in coresponsibility with the whole episcopal body united to its head. Doubtless, the magisterium must take account of the common belief of the faithful before pronouncing itself. But the episcopal college has not only the mission of recording this faith as it is lived, it must also discern the elements of this faith and pass judgment on them. And this judgment is binding on the consciences of the bishops as well as upon the faithful.

In the context of these clarifications, the question of a greater or less democratization in the method of the church's government remains a valid one. The solution to this question cannot but influence the status of the layman in the church of tomorrow.

COMMON RESPONSIBILITY

"God has gathered together as one all those who in faith look upon Jesus as the author of salvation and the source of unity and peace, and has established them as the church, that for each and for all she may be the visible sacrament of this saving unity." (*Constitution on the Church,* art. 9). Universal perspectives characterize the description of the church given by this conciliar constitution; whether it be question of the church as a sacrament or as a mystery or as the people of God, the first reality that meets our view is this vision of the Christian community as a whole.

The first and as it were primordial responsibility of the church is this *common* witness, this *common* priesthood,

192

this *common* holiness, which comes from each one and from all at the same time.

There is a common witness. It is the Christian community as such which must shed the light enlightening all men, which must announce the good news, the call to follow Christ and proclaim his message and his beatitudes. By its life and its actions, by its very existence "in the Spirit," the community of the faithful is the sign witnessing to the new Israel.

There is a common priesthood. The Christian community as such exercises that fundamental and common mediatory function which the Lord has raised up in this world for the sake of the world. It is this community which is the sacrament of unity and union, the praise of universal adoration and the instrument of salvation and redemption for the whole human community.

There is a common holiness. Once again it is the community of the faithful as such which must assure the victory of good over evil, of life over sin, and of Christ over Satan. It is the spouse of Christ who is holy. And even if at any given moment this holiness is "still imperfect" (*Constitution on the Church,* art. 48), the church nevertheless possesses the promises of Christ, that "she is beyond the grasp of the serpent's head" (see Apoc. 12, 14).

Consequently, the dominant characteristic of the Christian people is the communal aspect, with all the psychological and pastoral demands that this implies. Let us listen to Pope Paul VI:

> The note of community constantly affirmed in the documents of the council deserves to be studied. Such a study would confirm this truly ecclesial aspect, that is, this community aspect which should characterize the society of those who believe in Christ. . . .

193

Consequently, someone nourishes the spirit of the council when he attempts to introduce into Catholic life greater union, fraternity and love. Whatever lessens or injures the sense of community is outside the direction which the council has marked out for the renewal and growth of the church. Any sort of particularism, or egoism, any pretensions, which sometimes find their way into certain people or certain groups of catholics, or even a lack of interest in our brothers whether they be close or far away, must now after the council give way to this spirit of greater fraternal love which Christ willed to be the distinctive characteristic of his disciples.[1]

At this primary level, if we can use the expression, there exists a radical equality of rank among all the disciples of the Lord. "There are no more distinctions between Jew and Greek, slave and free, male and female, but all of you are one man in Jesus Christ" (Gal. 3, 28). All are called to the same unique holiness (see *Constitution on the Church,* art. 40).

All of Christ's faithful, therefore, whatever be the conditions, duties and circumstances of their lives, will grow in holiness day by day through these very situations, if they accept all of them with faith from the hand of their heavenly Father, and if they cooperate with the divine will by showing every man through their earthly activities the love with which God has loved the world (*Constitution on the Church,* art. 41).

But this fundamental equality is not a mass-produced identity. To the degree that grace is accepted, in the measure of each individual's holiness, there is a scale of spiritual values at the top of which there are those who are the most holy in the eyes of the Lord. There is a spiritual hierarchy, so to speak, still invisible on this earth. But

1. Address to General Audience, December 29, 1965.

this is the primordial hierarchy because it establishes for-
ever differences in eternal life. This is the fundamental and
primary perspective of the church.

"Whatever you eat, whatever you drink, whatever you do
at all, do it for the glory of God" (1 Cor. 10, 31; see Col.
3, 17). This is the apostle's advice, his concept of the
Christian life. All those who, answering the call of the
Lord, commit themselves to live a Christian existence are
obviously called—except for a special vocation to the
ministry or to the practice of the evangelical counsels—
to live in the secular world. The "world" is not a special
place but the normal milieu of the ensemble of Christ's
disciples (see *Constitution on the Church,* art. 31). In
this sense, one could distinguish between "laity" and
"hierarchy."[2]

But what are the laity to do in the world? The *Constitution on the Church* (art. 34) answers clearly that "in the

2. In our modern languages, the Christian use of the term "world"
contains the same ambiguity that can be found, for instance, in the
Johannine writings: "All that is in the world, the desire of the flesh, the
desire of the eyes, the arrogance of power, is not from the Father, it is
from the world" (1 Jn. 2, 16); and: "God loved the world so much
that he gave his only Son, so that everyone who believes in him may
not be lost but may have eternal life" (Jn. 3, 16). When we describe
the role of the laymen "in the world," our terminology is not meant to
imply that clerics are in a different geographical locality or that there
is something "holy" in itself about having less to do with the present
realities of human existence. We refer rather to those two "realms"
which, though distinct, "are so connected in the one plan of God that
he himself intends in Christ to appropriate the whole universe into a
new creation, initially here on earth, fully on the last day" (*Decree on
the Apostolate of the Laity,* art. 5).

spirit of God" they must live all their occupations and activities, their prayers and apostolic endeavors, their conjugal and family life, their daily work, the relaxation of their body, the leisure of their mind, their sufferings and trials. This, fundamentally, constitutes the "spiritual offerings" and the spiritual cult which they must give to God. This constitutes the very stuff of their common priesthood. Earlier in the same constitution we find the same perspective briefly sketched out for us:

> The baptized, by regeneration and the anointing of the Holy Spirit, are consecrated into a spiritual house and a holy priesthood. Thus through all those works befitting Christian men they can offer spiritual sacrifices and proclaim the power of him who has called them out of darkness into his marvelous light (art. 10).

To say the same thing more simply, these conciliar documents are saying to the laymen: in the Spirit, that is, in the state of grace, live out your daily existence, work and leisure, conjugal life and family existence, prayers and apostolic efforts. All of this is fundamentally your spiritual cult, your common priesthood. All of your activities, whether they be "profane" or "religious," if they are lived "in the Spirit" possess a deep meaning. They are offerings and sacrifices, they are doctrinal witness, they pertain to your royal priesthood.

But let it be well understood, these activities pertain to the business of being a man; they are, to use some expressions of the *Constitution on the Church in the Modern World,* those "labors and native endowments by which man has ceaselessly striven to better his life" (art. 33). They constitute the drive present in man "to subject to himself the earth and all that it contains, and to govern the world

196

with justice and holiness" (art. 34). They include "all that men do to obtain greater justice, wider brotherhood, and a more humane ordering of social relationships . . ." (art. 35).

The Christian community as it lives out its daily existence according to God becomes within the heart of the world, and for the sake of the world, a sign of the Lord, a light, a power, a ferment.

> For after we have obeyed the Lord, and in his Spirit nurtured on earth the values of human dignity, brotherhood and freedom, and indeed all the good fruits of our nature and enterprise, we will find them again, but freed of stain, burnished and transfigured. This will be so when Christ hands over to the Father a kingdom eternal and universal: "a kingdom of truth and life, of holiness and grace, of justice, love, and peace" (art. 39).

RELATIONS BETWEEN LAITY AND HIERARCHY

When we consider the relationships binding the laity to the pastors of the church, we must distinguish different domains, for there is a great diversity of situations.

When there is question of technical or scientific activity we should and must defend that autonomy of which the *Constitution on the Church in the Modern World* speaks.

> If by the autonomy of earthly affairs we mean that created things and societies themselves enjoy their own laws and values which must be gradually deciphered, put to use and regulated by men, then it is entirely right to demand that autonomy. Such is not merely required by modern man, but harmonizes also with the will of the Creator. For by the very circumstances of their having been created, all things are endowed with their own stability, truth, goodness, proper laws and order. Man must respect these as he isolates

197

them by the appropriate methods of the individual sciences or arts (art. 36).

When one approaches the domain of human realities, it is certain that the contribution of the shepherds of the church can add light. But the more that a situation touches upon human conduct and the natural law, the more it behooves these shepherds to be prudent and to remember what they themselves declared at the council precisely in regard to the laity.

Laymen should also know that it is generally the function of their well-formed Christian conscience to see that the divine law is inscribed in the life of the earthly city. From priests they may look for spiritual light and nourishment. Let the layman not imagine that his pastors are always such experts, that to every problem which arises, however complicated, they can readily give him a concrete solution, or even that such is their mission. Rather, enlightened by Christian wisdom and giving close attention to the teaching authority of the church, let the layman take his own distinctive role (art. 43).

When there is question of the life of prayer, the sacraments or of the liturgy, it is obvious that the Lord's ministers have a special place and fulfill a special role, even if all the baptized can also exercise a certain cultic activity well described in the *Constitution on the Church in the Modern World* (art. 11). Nevertheless, the concrete manner of regulating and organizing the whole of the liturgical and cultic life can and ought to be decided in union with the whole Christian society. The "power" of the priesthood, whether one considers it as a "prerogative" or a "service," does not confer *ipso facto* all the qualities necessary for the organization of the whole liturgical life. Here too the competence proper to each one should come into play and be recognized.

There are, finally, "apostolic activities" ranging from casual conversation and daily conduct, up to the share taken in tasks which pertain more specifically to the pastors of the Christian people. In each case, the Christian faith is operative in some degree. Christians themselves should check, revise and criticize the value of their commitment. But to the degree that their apostolic activities approach those which are confided to the hierarchy, lay people are more obliged to be and remain fully loyal and docile to the hierarchy.

There are many forms of the apostolate according to the *Decree on the Apostolate of the Laity*. "There are many apostolic undertakings which are established by the free choice of the laity, and regulated by their prudent judgment" (art. 24). The document also states: "Because of the demands of the common good of the Church, ecclesiastical authority can select and promote in a particular way some of the apostolic associations and projects which have an immediately spiritual purpose, thereby assuming in them a special responsibility" (art. 24). And, "Finally, the hierarchy entrusts to the laity some functions which are more closely connected with pastoral duties, such as the teaching of Christian doctrine, certain liturgical actions, and the care of souls. By virtue of this mission, the laity are fully subject to higher ecclesiastical direction in the performance of such work" (art. 24).

There is, then, a whole gamut of possible situations which evokes an equally varied gamut of relations between the laity and the hierarchy. The conciliar documents have traced out their general characteristics.[3] In reality, we must be able to avail ourselves of many possibilities. There is no uniform conduct to be observed by the pastor in regard to the laity or the laity in regard to the pastor.

Having said this, we wish to go on now to point out in a particular way certain characteristics of the apostolate of the laity which express an especially intimate coresponsibility with the pastors of the church.

THE TWOFOLD TASK OF LAYMEN

For a theology of the layman to be adequate, it must take account of the dual situation of the layman who is at once in the world and in the church. It is important to note that the laity have a twofold task which is proper to them: to christianize the temporal sphere, and to evangelize the world. As a citizen of the earthly city, the Christian layman must cause the gospel to permeate the context of the world in which he lives, and to give life to its structures. But then, as a citizen of the city of God, it pertains to him also to take a part in the visible extension of the kingdom of God here below, to be a witness of his faith in word and in action. There is a certain kind of apostolate which at times can be too pietistic and disconnected with life. In reaction against it there is a tendency so to incarnate the apostolate of the laity within the realities of this world that we run the risk of enclosing it completely in the sphere of the temporal. The balance between transcendence and immanence must be embodied in all Christian life, and thus too in the Christian apostolate.

3. Cf. *Dogmatic Constitution on the Church*, Arts. 36–37; *Decree on the Apostolate of the Laity*, Arts. 24–26.

Speaking of the necessary presence of the Christian in the world, the council said in its *Decree on the Apostolate of the Laity:*

Christ's redemptive work, while of itself directed toward the salvation of men, involves also the renewal of the whole temporal order. Hence the mission of the church is not only to bring to men the message and grace of Christ, but also to penetrate and perfect the temporal sphere with the spirit of the gospel. In fulfilling this mission of the Church, the laity therefore exercise their apostolate both in the Church and in the world, in both the spiritual and the temporal orders. These realms, although distinct, are so connected in the one plan of God that he himself intends in Christ to appropriate the whole universe into a new creation, initially here on earth, fully on the last day. In both orders, the layman, being simultaneously a believer and a citizen, should be constantly led by the same Christian conscience (art. 5).

Then, speaking of the cooperation of the laity in the work of evangelization, the council declared:

The mission of the Church concerns the salvation of men, which is to be achieved by belief in Christ and by his grace. Hence the apostolate of the Church and of all her members is primarily designed to manifest Christ's message by words and deeds and to communicate his grace to the world. This work is done mainly through the ministry of the word and of the sacraments, which are entrusted in a special way to the clergy. But the laity too have their very important roles to play if they are to be "fellow workers for the truth" (3 Jn. 8). It is especially on this level that the apostolate of the laity and the pastoral ministry complement one another.

There are innumerable opportunities open to the laity for the exercise of their apostolate of making the gospel known and men holy. The very testimony of their Christian life, and good works done in a supernatural spirit, have the power to draw men to belief and to God; for the Lord says, "Even so let your light shine before men, in order that they may see your good works and give glory to your Father in heaven" (Mt. 5, 16).

However, an apostolate of this kind does not consist only in the witness of one's way of life; a true apostle looks for opportunities to announce Christ by words addressed either to nonbelievers with a view to leading them to faith, or to believers with a view to instructing and strengthening them, and motivating them toward a more fervent life. "For the love of Christ impels us" (2 Cor. 5, 14), and the words of the apostle should echo in every Christian heart: "For woe to me if I do not preach the gospel" (1 Cor. 9, 16).

Since, in this age of ours, new problems are arising and extremely serious errors are gaining currency which tend to undermine the foundations of religion, the moral order and human society itself, this sacred Synod earnestly exhorts laymen, each according to his natural gifts and learning, to be more diligent in doing their part according to the mind of the Church, to explain and defend Christian principles, and to apply them rightly to the problems of our era (art. 6).

Thus the council earnestly invites laymen to assume fully the prophetic mission which is theirs as witnesses of the faith in the world. If the task of preaching the gospel was confided to the people of God as a whole, then certainly the laity, by far the greater number of this people, have a great part of the coresponsibility implied in maintaining, spreading and increasing the faith which they are called to live and preach.

To help them fulfill this role, it seems to us that it is important that all understand to what a degree the faith of the people of God, a faith which grows in prayer and love, is a community reality, a wealth of life in which we all share.

202

Church Faith

Before being an individual commitment binding the soul directly to God, faith is a commitment to God lived out in communion with the living church. The faith of each believer passes through the mediation of the church, and it is the church as a mother which brings us to birth in the faith.

When a child is brought to baptism, the priest asks this question: "What do you ask of the church of God?" In responding "Faith" we ask to be admitted into the faith of the church. The child is baptized into the faith of his parents, within a family. "He and all his household believed," the gospel tells us in regard to the nobleman whose son was healed (Jn. 4, 53). The family is the first sanctuary, the first "domestic church" (*Constitution on the Church,* art. 11). From the very beginning of our commitment, directly if it be an adult, indirectly if it be an infant, there is a community which receives us, for it is together that we are meant to live the mystery of God taking possession of man.

As Paul Ricoeur has well said, "Faith is a 'we' not an 'I'." He goes on to add: "It is this 'we' which possesses the aspect of handing on, of 'tradition' in the original meaning of the phrase. . . . Preaching has as its function that it be heard by many . . . the dialectic of conviction and responsibility must be supported by the deeper dialectic of the ecclesial and the social."[4]

This "church faith" is such a fundamental reality that it

4. P. Ricoeur, "Sciences humaines et conditionnement de la foi" in *Dieu aujourd'hui,* Paris, 1965, pp. 140–141.

is the recipient of the Lord's promise of indefectibility. Let us listen to the council on this subject:

> The body of the faithful as a whole, anointed as they are by the Holy One, cannot err in matters of belief. Thanks to a supernatural sense of the faith which characterizes the people as a whole, it manifests this unerring quality when, from the bishops down to the last member of the laity, it shows universal agreement in matters of faith and morals (*Constitution on the Church,* art. 12).

THE SENSE OF THE FAITHFUL

The sense of the faithful, that rectitude of judgment, which permits them to "test and interpret all things in a truly Christian spirit" (*Modern World,* art. 62), is a reality which finds its place in the hierarchical communion and bears its stamp. It is an active thing, a sort of supernatural instinct which aids in discerning the Holy Spirit at work in the church.

Pope Paul VI indicated the importance of this sense of the faithful within the work of theology itself:

> Sacred theology has a twofold relationship with the church's magisterium and with the worldwide community of Christians. First, it holds a sort of midway position between the faith of the church and the church's magisterium. It earnestly seeks to discover how the Christian community might translate its faith into practice, and it tries to grasp the truths, opinions, questions, and tendencies which the Holy Spirit stirs up in the people of God: "what the Spirit says to the churches" (Apoc. 2, 7).
>
> Using the methods and principles proper to its field, sacred theology must evaluate the faith of God's people as actually lived, and their aims, in order to bring them into harmony with the word

204

of God and the doctrinal heritage faithfully handed down by the Church. . . .

Cultivating the spirit of communion is part of the very essence of the Christian vocation, as the apostle John teaches. But in a particular way it is an essential part of a sound theological outlook and approach.

Divine truth is preserved in the whole Christian community by the Holy Spirit. Hence within this community you will find truth more easily, if you cultivate closer ties of communion with the entire community of the faithful; if you emulate the humility of the little ones, to whom our heavenly Father more readily reveals His mysterious nature and his hidden designs.[5]

Cardinal Dechamps, archbishop of Maline, and one of the prominent figures at Vatican I, used to express in his own way an identical thought, by saying that simple people believe for good reasons, and leave to the better educated the duty of showing that these reasons are good.

It even happens that this sense of the faithful, of which the pope makes so much, can precede theological work and provide it with a fundamental intuition. It suffices to think here of the long history of the proclamation of the dogma of the immaculate conception in which the sense of the faithful was finally joined, after laborious discussion, by the assent of theologians and the ratification of the magisterium.

This sense of the faithful which we have just seen at work in the truths of faith can be seen equally at work when it comes to discerning holiness, which is nothing else than a fully lived life of faith. At one time canonizations were accomplished by a sort of plebiscite, "*Vox populi, vox Dei.*" Then in the 13th century, in order to avoid abuses, canonization was reserved to the Holy See, though today once

5. Address of Paul VI to International Congress on the Theology of Vatican II.

again the intuitions of the Christian people in regard to a "servant of God" play an important role in his canonization, and this role could be augmented.

The more that a canonization derives from an expression of the Christian people, the more the figure of a saint corresponds to an ideal of a successful Christian in the eyes of his milieu and age, the more powerful an invitation it is for the rest of the people of God.

At the council, we made a few suggestions in regard to adaptations in the process of canonizations. It is sufficient here without entering into details to point out the value and efficacy of this sense of the faithful when it comes to discerning sanctity.

The sense of the faithful is not a sort of human public opinion, dominated by the ebb and flow and fashions of the day. It results from the action of the Holy Spirit who is the soul of the church and the source of its charisms. Beside or rather within the hierarchical structure of the church there is room for a manifold supernatural activity of the Spirit who confers his charisms and gifts with a view toward rendering the church of God more alive and more beautiful. This charismatic dimension of the church is of central importance in ecumenical dialogue, whether it be with our Orthodox brothers, or our brothers of the reform, both of whom are so sensitive to the pneumatic aspect of Christian life. The church, in asking the faithful to accept their full and prophetic coresponsibility in the world, knows well that the Holy Spirit is at work to accomplish in and through them his great designs.[6]

6. The text of my intervention at the council on the charismatic dimension of the church may be found as an appendix to this chapter.

206

CORESPONSIBLE IN THE FAITH

St. John summons all the faithful to be "co-workers in the truth." For the faithful to respond to this invitation, they must have a living awareness of faith's primacy in their lives, and know their duties in regard to it.

In an age of pragmatism and utilitarianism, there is a great temptation to put action ahead of thought, to value efficiency more than doctrinal solidity, and to pay attention to what is easier rather than what is most necessary. However, today as yesterday, nothing is more important than discovering the truth of God and that which it has to tell us about man and the world. We are told to "do the truth in love." We must have a light which can point out the road, otherwise we will wander in the darkness. In one of his books, E. Hello has one of his characters ask the question, "What is the most important thing for man so that he may not die of hunger?" The answer came back, "Bread." "No," replied the wise man, "his greatest need is the sun," and he goes on to explain that without the sun there would be no grain, no harvest, no bread in the oven or on the table. What is most necessary for a Christian, that his Christian life not die? Above all he needs the truth of God, the truth which enlightens every man coming into the world. The gospel shows us that the greatest sin is not the sin of the flesh, but a sin against the light. The first duty of any believer is to live in contact with this truth of God, to maintain his vision of faith in all its clarity, to keep his baptized mind in the light.

But respect for the faith means not only that we keep it intact, but that we nourish it and allow it to grow "up to the stature of the full measure of Christ." We would blush

207

to find that our knowledge of profane things had simply vegetated and remained at an elementary level, but we easily adjust to having our religious knowledge stay stunted at a child's level, or at least at a stage well inferior to that of our knowledge of other things. It is easy to see the danger of such a gap: an atrophied faith is a faith in danger. To remain indifferent to our religious culture is neither logical nor legitimate. We have less excuse than ever in an age where the daily press, magazines, television and radio constantly air religious problems, and in which error and ignorance in matters of faith and morals daily meet our ears and enter our souls. How is it possible without a religious culture worthy of its name for us to rectify these things for ourselves or for others?

Ignorance in matters of religion is the greatest cause of dechristianization. A layman whose faith is ill informed finds himself helpless to resist the constant attrition caused by waves of discrepant ideologies, opinions and moralities. Pius XII relied heavily on the young for the future of religion. He counted upon the reaction of their critical spirit. But how could anyone insufficiently enlightened be capable of such discernment? He is like some unprotected beach open to all the action of the tides.

It would be interesting to ask the educated faithful questions such as "How many religious books have you read this year, in order to maintain and nourish your faith?" "What Christian weekly, or quarterly, do you read, in order to stay informed about the life of the church?" "How much time have you given in your life to making retreats, taking courses of renewal, going to lectures which treat of religion?" All too often the answers would be discouraging. But how in such conditions can Christians be witnesses to

208

that faith of which the world stands in need? How can they be "children of the light," servants of a word of God which they do not know themselves? John Courtney Murray used to say, "It is dangerous to read unsuitable books, but it is worse not to read good ones."

All the faithful should develop their faith by prayer, reading and study. But there is room within the people of God for a certain type of layman, too rare among us, the lay theologian. In the early centuries of Christianity lay theologians were not rare. We find men such as Justin Martyr, Lactantius, Didymus the Blind and Aristides of Athens, to mention only some great figures of the early church.

How did it happen in the Latin church that theology became a clerical monopoly, while in the Orthodox and reform churches there are lay theologians occupying university chairs in theology? Why is this "faith looking for understanding," which is the definition of theology, a special reserve of clerics? The treasures which it contains are available for all who can and will search them out.

The lay theologian is particularly qualified to engage in the dialogue between faith and science, between faith and the moral, philosophical, social and political ideals of this new world coming into being before our eyes. Today we do find many laymen beginning to treat of theological questions; some of them give expression to a profound life of faith and real professional competence in their given field. It is a welcome sight to see such men assume their responsibility and enter into a domain which we in the Western church

209

have incorrectly considered to be the fief of clerics. If rather than be content with juxtaposing their faith and their profession, those believers who are engaged at university level were to try to integrate these two dimensions of their soul and give expression to this integration, the faith of the rest of the people of God would be greatly enlightened.

"CO-WORKERS IN THE TRUTH"

But even if we do not go so far and think of expert theologians, there is still a great role for enlightened lay people, especially those who in one way or another are connected with the field of communications, whether they be writers, journalists or publishers. These could make an irreplaceable contribution if they were able to transmit their Christian perspectives regarding events of the world with a style in keeping with their professional techniques. Events are speaking to us. We must be able to read the signs of the times, and give them their correct meaning. We need what we would like to call a "theology of the actual," which is nothing more than a Christian gaze upon what is happening at the moment and its interpretation. There is a constant dialogue between the world and the church. Laymen who are rooted in this world are more able than anyone else to find a way of speaking to it. But this presupposes a living faith, a faith that is on the alert and able to make its witness. "I believed, therefore I spoke."

The layman who assumes his coresponsibility for the prophetic mission of the church can bring to his task specific contributions which have great consequences for the life of the church itself. His training, his professional competence, his manifold field of interests can enrich and modify beyond measure the role of the church in the world.

The attitude of the layman in regard to the church should be active and ready to collaborate rather than passive and inert. The words of John Kennedy to the youth of America come readily to mind: "Ask not what your country can do for you, but what you can do for your country." The layman should ask this kind of question of the church. For the church is not something extrinsic to him, something which he can meet and help at times. The church is himself, he is the church. It was the understanding of this identity that inspired the council to create in every diocese in the world a diocesan pastoral council, composed of priests, religious and laymen in order to utilize and express the reality of their coresponsibility.

All too often in times gone by, recourse was had to the laity specifically in regard to financial matters, where their competence was obvious and precious. But the potential for collaboration is immeasurably greater than this. They must help in elaborating the general orientation of pastoral activity within a diocese, an area of life or a parish. Because of their professions and their daily experience, laymen know how to draw the greatest profit from teamwork. They know its practical problems and how to update institutions which are proving ineffectual. We need the competence of our administrators, the knowledge of those engaged in law and teaching, the talent of our writers, the sense of social justice of our labor leaders. We wish to be helped by the practical insights of our sociologists, as well as the professional competence of our city planners and architects in order to have a realistic pastoral effort in our ever growing urban

211

areas. And we await the wisdom of our doctors, psychologists and psychiatrists in bringing the word of God to bear on the modern problems of family, marriage and education. Briefly, the church stands in need of a widespread exercise of apostolic coresponsibility on the part of the laity. The World Congress of the Lay Apostolate which ended in October 1967 at Rome dramatically showed that the people of God are becoming aware of this need, and have shown signs of a promise rich for the future.

Conclusion

At the end of these pages we hope that it has become somewhat clearer how responsible all Christians are, as a body, for their Christianity. The way that this collegiality will be lived out will condition the future of the church, especially in regard to our missionary and ecumenical hopes. The collegial notion is deeply engraved in the tradition of the church, and by that very fact it is a determining element of the future. Claudel compared tradition to a man walking: he must have one foot on the ground and the other in movement if he wishes to go ahead. The church makes its way toward the future in a living continuity with the past, but this continuity is neither conservativism nor servility, it is fidelity. The sense of coresponsibility must be the soul of the apostolic activity of the 20th century, and of the centuries which follow.

Resolutely utilizing all the charismatic wealth of the people of God, the church will be more authentically than ever before the church of Pentecost. The Spirit of God animates the church with a view to renewing constantly

212

its youth. A young church is by that very fact adapted to the young world which we experience being born. The young Christians of today who will play their part in making the world of the year 2000 are growing up in a climate of widespread renewal. The world which will be theirs will not be merely a new phase of an old world, but, if we can believe all the indications, it will be a truly new world.

The church must be receptive to the values of the future, to the genuine riches of this world being born, so that Christ, who is the king of ages, may purify these realities, take them to himself and transform them. Someone once said that young people are a radar set helping us to see what is coming. It is most important that the church truly dialogue with the young, and understand their new awareness. As Paul Valéry has said, "Youth prophesies by its very existence, being what it will be." Because of this contact the church will better understand that it must renew its style of life in order the better to hand on the word of life confided to it. The more that the Holy Spirit lives in each one of us the more he will be able to reveal to the men of tomorrow the youth, the freshness and the power of the gospel. The more profoundly he will be the creator-Spirit who renews the face of the earth.

Appendix to Chapter IX

There has been very little mention of the charisms of Christ's faithful, and this could create the impression that they are a peripheral or accidental phenomenon in the life of the church. But we should point out more explicitly the vital importance of these charisms for the building up of the mystical body.

We must take care that the hierarchical structure of the church does not appear as an administrative apparatus having no intimate connection with the charismatic gifts of the Holy Spirit to be found throughout the church.

The time of the church, which is making its way through the ages up to the parousia of the Lord, is the time of the Holy Spirit. For it is through this Holy Spirit that the glorified Christ unites, purifies, vivifies and brings into the total truth the eschatological people of God, despite the weaknesses and sins of this people. The Holy Spirit is thus the first fruits (Rom. 8, 23) and the pledge of the Church (2 Cor. 1, 22).

Thus it follows that the Holy Spirit is not given only to the pastors of the church, but to all Christians. "Do you not know that you are the temple of God and that the Spirit of God dwells in you?" St. Paul asked the Corinthians (1 Cor. 3, 16). Every Christian receives the Holy Spirit at baptism which is the sacrament of faith. All Christians are the "living stones" called to be used in the building up of a "spiritual edifice" (1 Pet. 2, 5). That is why the whole church is by its nature a truly spiritual reality, a building whose foundation is not only the apostles, but, according to Ephesians 2, 20, also the prophets. In the church of the New Testament Christ has given "some to be apostles, some prophets, some evangelists, others pastors, and teachers" (Eph. 4, 11; see 3, 5).

The Holy Spirit manifests himself in the church by the number and richness of the spiritual gifts, called in the scriptures gifts of the Spirit (1 Cor. 12, 1; 14, 1) or charisms (Rom. 12, 6; 1 Cor. 12, 4. 9. 28. 30 ff.; 1 Tim. 4, 14; 2 Tim. 1, 6; 1 Pet. 4, 10). It is true that in the time of St. Paul some charismatic gifts were evident in the church in a dramatic and surprising way. There was the "gift of tongues" (1 Cor. 12, 10. 28. 30; 14, 18. 26; Acts 19, 6) or the gift of healing (1 Cor. 12, 9. 28. 30; see 1 Cor. 12, 10. 12. 28 ff; Gal. 3, 5), but we should never think that the gifts of the Spirit are exclusively and principally in these phenomena which are rather extraordinary and uncommon.

St. Paul spoke, for instance, of the charism of the word of wisdom and knowledge (1 Cor. 12, 8), of the charism of faith (1 Cor. 12, 9), the charisms of teaching (Rom. 12, 7; 1 Cor. 12, 28 ff.; 14, 26), of exhorting or consoling (Rom. 12, 8), of service (Rom. 12, 7), the charism of discerning spirits (1 Cor. 12, 10), and the charisms of social aid and leadership (1 Cor. 12, 28), and of others as well.

Thus for St. Paul the church of Christ was not just an administrative organization but an organic and living reality made up of gifts, charisms and services. The Spirit is given to all Christians, and to each one in particular. He confers on each his gifts and charisms which "differ according to the grace given us" (Rom. 12, 6).

"The manifestation of the Spirit is given to each one for the common good" (1 Cor. 12, 7), that is, for the "building up of the church" (1 Cor. 14, 12). Every Christian, educated or simple, has his gift in his daily life, but as St. Paul says again, "Everything must work to build up" (1 Cor. 14, 26; see 14, 3–5). The apostle also affirms that God has established "First, apostles, then prophets, thirdly teachers . . . are all apostles, are all prophets, or teachers?" (1 Cor. 12, 28).

A schema on the church which would speak only of the apostles and their successors, and not mention equally prophets and teachers, would be deficient in a most important regard. What would become of our church without the charisms of its teachers and theologians? What would it be without the charisms of its prophets or of men who speak under inspiration of the Spirit? For these men who speak out "in season and out of season" (2 Tim. 4, 2) come to the aid of a church which is sometimes slumbering so that gospel of Christ is not neglected in practice.

The church of today is not lacking in the charism of teachers, prophets and other ministries, any more than in former ages, or in the time of St. Thomas Aquinas and St. Francis of Assisi. May it not be lacking also these gifts in her daily and ordinary life.

But let us put to one side the more "dramatic" charisms and consider the "more simple" gifts. Does not each and every one of us here know of laymen and laywomen in his own diocese who are truly called by God? They are endowed by the Spirit with various charisms in the fields

216

of catechetics, evangelization, apostolic action in all its ramifications, in social work and charitable activity. Does not our daily experience provide us with proof that the activity of the Holy Spirit is not extinct in the church?

Certainly, without the ministry of the pastors, the charisms of the church would be aberrant. But on the other hand, without these charisms, the ecclesiastical ministry would be impoverished and sterile. It pertains to the pastors of the local churches or the pastor of the universal church to discern these charisms of the Spirit by a spiritual intuition, and to nourish and increase them. '

It pertains to the pastors of the church to listen carefully and with open hearts to the lay people who so often enter into dialogue with them. For lay people, each and every one of them, are endowed with their own gifts and charisms and often have a greater experience of the life of the world today.

Finally, the pastors themselves are called to desire the "greater gifts" (1 Cor. 12, 31). Of course, all the faithful, even those possessed of great gifts, owe respect to their pastors. But then, reciprocally, there should be equal attention and respect paid to the charisms and movements of the Holy Spirit, for he often breathes within the Christian people, and not only within the pastors. "Never suppress the Spirit or treat the gift of prophecy with contempt; think before you do anything—hold on to what is good . . ." (1 Thes. 5, 19–21). This organic and living reality made up of gifts, charisms and services cannot be achieved and cannot work for the building up of the church without the liberty of the sons of God. This liberty should be protected and encouraged by all the pastors, following the example of St. Paul.

217

In conclusion: on the doctrinal level we would propose that the chapter treating of the people of God be perfected according to what has just been said.

(1) That the charismatic dimension of the church be carefully defined, at the same time as the structure of its ministry.

(2) That the importance of charisms within the people of God be given a greater and more concrete emphasis.

(3) That in particular the importance of prophets and teachers in the church be examined.

(4) That the attitude of pastors in regard to charisms of the faithful be defined in a more positive and constructive way.

(5) That the doctrine of St. Paul on the liberty of the sons of God in the church, be not forgotten.

On the practical level, so that through the Holy Spirit our faith in the charisms given to all Christ's faithful be manifest at the council and in the eyes of all:

(1) May the number of lay auditors increase, and may these express broader fields of representation.

(2) May even women be invited. If I am not mistaken, they constitute half of humanity.

(3) Finally, may religious brothers and sisters be invited, for they too belong to the people of God. They receive the Holy Spirit and serve the Church as an elect portion of the Lord's flock.